COCKLES OF THE HEART

Marion Halligan was born in Newcastle on the east coast of Australia and grew up by the sea. She now lives in Canberra, with her husband and, occasionally, two children. Her books have been nominated for most of the major literary prizes and have won several, including the Steele Rudd Award (for best collection of short stories in its year), the Braille Book of the Year for *The Living Hothouse*, and the Geraldine Pascal Prize for critical writing. Her novel, *Lovers' Knots*, won the *Age* Book of the Year Award, the ACT Book of the Year Award, the 3M Talking Book of the Year Award and the inaugural Nita B Kibble Literary Award.

Her other books are the novels *Self-Possession, Spider Cup* and *Wishbone*, two more collections of short stories, *The Hanged Man in the Garden* and *The Worry Box*, and *Eat My Words*, a collection of essays about food and other things.

She has published over sixty short stories in journals and magazines, and has been widely anthologised.

COCKLES OF THE HEART

Marion Halligan

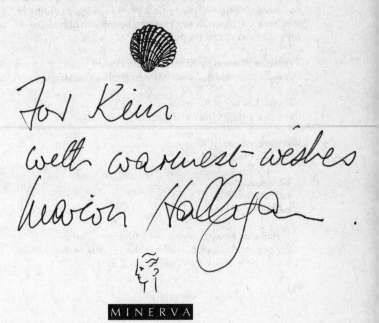

For Kim
with warmest wishes
Marion Halligan.

MINERVA

Published 1996 by Minerva
a part of Reed Books Australia
22 Salmon Street, Port Melbourne, Victoria 3207
a division of Reed International Books Australia Pty Limited

Typeset in Palatino by Abbtypesetting Pty Ltd
Printed and bound in Australia by Australian Print Group

National Library of Australia
cataloguing-in-publication data:

Halligan, Marion, 1940–.
   Cockles of the heart.

   Bibliography.
   Includes index.
   ISBN 1 86330 519 X.

   1. Halligan, Marion, 1940–. — Journeys — Europe.
   2. Authors, Australian — 20th century — Journeys — Europe.
   3. Europe — Description and travel. I. Title.

914

For Lucy and James

Acknowledgements

Thanks to Cosmo, Lucy, James, Bernard, Grant, Catherine, Etienne, Judy, Neil, Nancy, Robert, and Carol for consenting to be characters in my narratives.

Thanks to G.J. Halligan for translations from *La Chanson de Roland*.

Thanks to Damien Pignolet of Bistro Moncur for his recipe for *brandade de morue*.

Thanks to Margaret Connolly who makes agent synonymous with friend.

And with gratitude to the Literature Board of the Australia Council for the grants that have made my writing life possible.

The recipe for *île flottant* is my translation from *La Cuisine de Madame Saint-Ange*, Editions Chaix, 1977.

GLOSSARY

Barthes, Roland (1915–80): French critic and semiotician. Books include *Mythologies*, *Writing Degree Zero*, *The Pleasure of the Text*.

Brillat-Savarin, Jean-Anthelme (1755–1826): French gastronome, author of *La Physiologie du Goût*, often translated as *The Philosopher in the Kitchen*, a book of aphorisms, anecdotes, theories, and recipes. He said: 'Tell me what a person eats and I will tell you what he is.'

Câreme (1784–1833): Chef and gastronome. He cooked for Talleyrand, George IV of England, the Austrian and Russian emperors. Wrote a number of books about cooking, and designed amazing set pieces that turned food into architecture, such as Chinese temples, Gothic palaces, hermits' grottos.

Colette (Sidonie Gabrielle) (1873–1954): French novelist, sometimes described as the most important woman novelist of the century. Books include the Claudine series and *La Chatte*. *Le Petit Robert* describes her prose as 'at once precise and savoury, almost gourmande'.

Escoffier, Auguste (1846–1935): French chef who gained his reputation in London, being one of the founders of the Savoy Hotel. He invented the *pêche Melba*.

Garbo, Greta (1905–90): Cinema actress, star of American films, born in Sweden. Famous for her classical beauty.

Mazout: A kind of fuel oil, used in stoves for heating and cooking.

Panhard: Family of engineers which was among the first manufacturers of cars in France. This driver seems to have been Rene, the founder of the company.

Reconquest: During the Middle Ages the Christians fought to drive the Moors out of Spain. They finally achieved this feat, which is called the Reconquest or *Reconquista* in Spanish, with the taking of Grenada in 1492.

Ronsard, Pierre (1524–85): A central figure of the French poetic renaissance, known for his light odes and lyric poems, especially sonnets.

Rouff, Marcel: Early twentieth-century author of *The Lives and Loves of Dodin Bouffant*, a gastronomic novel. A comic drama where food, the vicissitudes and pleasures associated with it, is the subject.

Sévigné, Marie de Rabutin-Chantal, Marquise de (Madame) (1626–96): An elegant and cultured noblewoman of great charm and intelligence, famous especially for her letters which are lively accounts of the daily life of the nobility, their social habits, domestic relations, and adventures.

Smith, Sydney (1771–1845): English clergyman and scholar, famous for his wit, especially in conversation but also in letters and reviews. Known for his recipe for salad in verse.

Talleyrand-Périgord, Charles-Maurice de (Prince) (1754–1838): French diplomat and bishop, known for his political genius and venality, whose skill in changing sides enabled him to survive from the Ancien Régime, through the Revolution and the period of Napoleon to the Restoration of the monarchy. As ambassador to England in 1830, he did much to shape the future of Europe.

Willy, or *Henri Gauthier-Villars* (1859–1931): Novelist and music-critic, who married Colette and published her first novels under his own pseudonym, Willy; in other words, she was his ghost-writer, or *nègre*.

A witty woman once said to me that she was able to tell gourmands by their pronunciation of the word good, in such phrases as 'That's good, that's very good,' etc; she declared that adepts instil into that one short monosyllable an accent of truth, tenderness, and enthusiasm such as ill-favoured palates can never attain.

The Philosopher in the Kitchen,
Jean-Anthelme Brillat-Savarin

… every man should eat and drink, and enjoy the good of all his labour, it is the gift of God.

Ecclesiastes, 111:13

THE PILGRIMAGE ROUTES

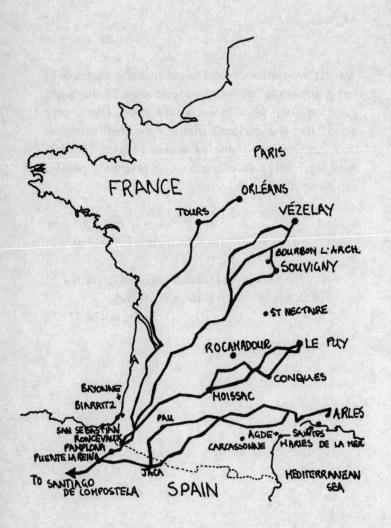

*The dinner table is the site of two most significant
human activities: the eating of food and the telling
of stories …*

To begin, some stories.

SARA AND THE GYPSIES

Once upon a time … a precise time, by and large,
about the year AD 40, a group of people was cast
adrift on the sea, in a boat without oars, without
sails, without provisions. Those aboard were Mary
Jacob, the sister of the Virgin Mary; Mary Salome,
mother of the apostles James the Elder and John;
Lazarus who rose from the dead, with his two
sisters, Martha and Mary Magdalene; Maximin
(whoever he is); and Sidoine who was cured of
blindness. A heavy load for a small boat. The aban-
doning was done by the Jews of Jerusalem, who
shortly before had crucified Christ.

One person was left behind: Sara, the black servant of the two Marys. She watched the boat float
away from the shore, full of despair, but Mary
Salome threw her mantle upon the water, where it
formed a raft, and carried Sara across the sea to the
boat.

Thanks to divine protection, the tiny craft came to
shore on a beach in Provence. There the passengers
separated, travelling their various ways, evangelising,

but not before building a rough oratory dedicated to the Virgin. The two Marys and Sara remained in the Camargue, and when they died the faithful placed their remains in the oratory. The tomb soon became the centre of a cult. Eventually a massive church was built, the church of Les Saintes Maries, the Holy Marys, and that is the name of the town, too — Saintes Maries de la Mer, the Holy Marys of the Sea. Wanderers especially are drawn here, the lean men, the black and silver cowboys of the Camargue, who ride wild horses and drive battered simple Citroens: the Gypsies and their handsome brown women continue to come to the church of Les Saintes Maries, they offer their prayers for future favours and thanks for past miracles to their patron saint, Sara, the black maid. For nineteen centuries they've been doing it, and show no signs of stopping.

FIELD OF STARS

Once upon a time … much the same as the last time. Another holy person crossed the ocean on a boat, a skiff, like that of the Marys, but in his case he went willingly. He was travelling to Spain to convert it. This was James the Elder, apostle of Christ, sonof Zebedee, former fisherman, nicknamed Son of Thunder because of his stormy temperament (or possibly because he was a bit of a wimp: take your pick). His skiff ran aground in the mouth of the River Ulla, in Galicia, much where the town of

Santiago de Compostela is now situated. For seven years he went up and down the country preaching, then returned to the Holy Land where he was beheaded by Herod Agrippa, and so became one of the earliest of Christian martyrs. This was in the Year of Our Lord 44.

After this the story branches. The plain version says that his disciples, being forced to leave Palestine, took his body to Spain and buried it near where they landed, on the same spot James ran aground all those years before.

Another version has his body placed in a boat with sails set, which next day reached the Spanish coast. The people of Padron, near Compostela, used to point to a huge stone as the actual craft.

My favourite has the relics of St James miraculously conveyed from Jerusalem, where he was bishop (bishops already!) to Spain in a marble ship. A knight saw the ship entering port. His horse took fright, possibly recognising how marvellous a thing is a marble ship, and plunged into the sea. The knight managed to save himself by climbing on board the vessel, when he found his clothes entirely covered with scallop-shells.

All these diverse stories converge again with the loss of the saint's remains. Every version agrees on that: so precious as they were, the relics were lost. Times were troubled. There were persecutions, Christians were forbidden to visit the tombs of saints. The barbarians and then the Arabs overran Spain, and people no longer remembered where James was buried.

Now the stories branch again. One says that a star revealed the place to some shepherds. This gives weight to the theory that the origin of the name Compostela is *campus stellae*, field of stars. Although the story of shepherds and stars seems to lack a little in originality. A later derivation, linked to the discovery of a necropolis under the cathedral, has the name coming from the low Latin *compostela*, meaning cemetery.

Another story has a hermit, in the year 813 — there's general agreement about the chronology of the finding — a hermit called Pelayo on the same spot observing lights and hearing music. Divine revelation occurs in both cases. He told his bishop, Theodimious, who discovered the remains, recognising them by the inscription on the tombstone. Proper ecclesiastical protocol is being observed here; the bishop told the king of Spain, who proclaimed James patron saint of his kingdom. The king built a basilica, which later became the cathedral.

Or perhaps it happened like this. Some thirty years later, the battle of Clavijo. Ramiro the Spanish king is fighting a Moorish army commanded by Abdar Rahman. It must not be forgotten that Spain is in the hands of the infidel. Suddenly a knight appears, mounted on a white horse, and carrying a standard with a red cross. Fighting on the side of the Spaniards. Thanks to him they win. The Christians realise that he is St James in person: Santiago Matamoros, St Jacques le Matamor, St James the Moor Killer. The Reconquest of Spain has found its patron. And its motto: *Santiago y Cierra Espana*, which is an exhortation to close Spain, to shut out the Moors. The same catchcry was taken up by Franco, who was always keen to associate himself with past glories wherever possible.

During this battle one of the knights is obliged to swim across an arm of the sea. He emerges covered in scallop-shells. Or cockle-shells you may call them. And so there is an emblem for St James.

I like this version. If you must choose a story, go for the most glamorous. Forget hierarchical propriety; it smacks of the meddling of bishops after the event. Marble ships and saints reincarnate have much more style.

Whichever you choose, it seems to be fact that it was in the eleventh century that Compostela took off as a shrine for Christians. Turkish invasions made the Holy Land too perilous, so they looked elsewhere, and saw Santiago on the western extremity of the known world, the *finis terrae*, the earth's end. Which in those days before Columbus Cape Finisterre was. Getting there looked good and difficult, a real trial, but not impossible, not suicidal.

Far-flung it is no longer, but still in the sights of Christians. And has been so for nine centuries, with only occasional periods of neglect. In the Middle Ages the route was called the Milky Way, because if you stood in France and looked at these stars, that's where they were pointing, it was as though you were walking along a road of stars. Charlemagne is supposed to have had a vision, to have looked up and seen the Milky Way and said, There at the end of that is a place of pilgrimage, which was rather clever of him, since the remains of St James hadn't yet been found, but you also have to wonder why he hadn't noticed this rather visible constellation before.

THE SPRING IN THE GROTTO

Once upon a time ... a time some eighteen centuries after the first story. A girl is collecting wood on the banks of a river. A mountain torrent. When she was born her father was a prosperous miller, but the advent of a steam mill in the district destroyed his livelihood and the family had to leave their pretty house by the stream, where they had lived in thrifty hard-working contentment. You could say they were victims of the industrial revolution. Now they are living in a stone hut, a disused prison no bigger than a shed. The parents hire themselves out as day labourers, but don't bring in enough money to feed the family. One day Bernadette, that's the child's name, finds her brother chewing on a church candle, he is so hungry.

So on this cold February day in 1858, by a bleak riverbank on the edge of the Pyrenees, the expedition of Bernadette and her sister and a friend in search of firewood is not for fun. It's survival. For a while she used to live in the country with her old wet nurse, as a servant, minding sheep and doing housework; at least that meant she was fed. But her mother has brought her back home to the stone hut not fit even for a prison in order to have her prepared for her first communion. Bernadette cannot read or write, she is a stunted child, sickly, wretched …

On the bank of a river is a cave, a hole in the cliff of rock where herds of pigs take shelter. Perhaps the children take shelter there, too. In the depths of this filthy hollow Bernadette sees a small girl, no bigger than herself. She is dressed in white, with a blue girdle, and a yellow rose on each foot. Over her arm she carries a string of rosary beads.

Eighteen times this beautiful person appears to Bernadette. On one occasion she asks her to kneel down on all fours, to kiss the ground, and scratch it. A thin spring of water spurts out. Bernadette drinks some, and washes her face, she eats some of the herbs growing beside it. By this time a great crowd is watching; news of the visitor has spread.

On another occasion the childish visitant identifies herself. I am the Immaculate Conception, she says, in the local patois: *Que soy era Immaculada Concepciou*. Bernadette's attention was drawn to her the first time by a rushing wind and a glow of light; the apparition invited her to pray. Later she asks Bernadette to come every day for a fortnight, and promises to make her happy not in this world, but in the next.

The doubtful priest of the village asks for a sign in order to believe in the Lady, this small person of the same height as undersized Bernadette: 140 centimetres, four feet eight inches, not very tall for a fourteen-year-old. He asks her to make a rose-bush bloom in February, and she does. The first cure happens on 1 March, of a paralysed hand plunged into the spring, which continued to flow and does so unabated to this day.

I like best Bernadette's comment on the Lady's words. *Voulez-vous me faire la grâce de venir ici pendant quinze jours*, the Lady asked. Would you do me the favour of coming here for fifteen days? Notice she says *vous*, the plural and polite form of you, not the singular *tu*, used to address intimates and inferiors. Bernadette said, The Lady was the first person who ever said *vous* to me.

That, far more than rose-bushes or hands unparalysed, would make you believe in Bernadette's small lady. That's the tiny detail that carries the weight of verisimilitude. That's the novelist's grain of truth, which can support a whole edifice of narrative.

These days five million people a year go to her town of Lourdes, seeking a miracle, a cure, illumination. And in the meantime Bernadette Soubirous, the illiterate sickly peasant girl, has become a saint.

SKELETONS

Books, like bodies, need skeletons. A skeleton might be a plot, or a theme, an idea. The writer might not always know what it is. *Eat My Words* was finished and between covers and out in the world before I realised that its skeleton was my autobiography. Not everything in it was autobiographical, but the bones were, and on them was hung the flesh, the muscles, the gristle, the veins and arteries carrying blood.

As any cook will tell you, you get more flavour from meat on the bone.

This time, I was clever before the event. I worked out what the skeleton of this book would be before I wrote it. A pilgrimage. Not the oldest, or the biggest, but probably the greatest. The pilgrimage to Santiago de Compostela, in Galicia, on the west coast of Spain, to the mighty cathedral of St James. A journey of architecture and food.

I once read a comment of Victor Hugo's, that architecture is the great handwriting of the human race. I fell in love with the handwriting on the land-scape when I spent time in that middle part of France where the churches are still Romanesque. We stayed in Sévérac in the house that a friend inher-ited from his grandfather's cousin, a house of many rooms and increasing comfort which we could live in whenever we pleased. We didn't have much money but we did have a car, and we'd load our-selves and the children into it and make trips into the countryside, sometimes taking a tent and going farther away, but always having as our object those marvellous letters written in stone six or eight or ten centuries ago, for whoever cared to read them. Often the churches are little more than chapels, plain and bare and heart-breakingly beauti-ful, hardly touched since their makers got them right nearly a millennium ago. Sometimes they are massive fortified piles, a spectacular forgetting of Christ's commandment to love one another.

Sometimes gorgeous cathedrals with treasures made of gold and cabochon emeralds, diamonds, rubies, to hold precious bits of saints, a finger, a thigh-bone, a tooth, or a little crystal phial of blood.

And the reason all of these are here: the pilgrimages coming from all over the known world to Compostela. The roads from all over Europe that wander their way through France before finally converging on the three passes that lead across the Pyrenees into Spain. Coming from Prague, Poland, Vienna, the German states, Scandinavia, England, Belgium. Look at the map and it is as though Europe is a giant funnel narrowing just past the Pyrenees into a single conduit, and all of Christendom pours down it. Through Vézelay, Conques, Moissac, Le Puy, St Gilles, St Guilhelm, depending on where you came from. You could go direct, or make detours among them. All great sites in their own right, and all linked by these routes like arteries branching back from the heart of Santiago. All the stages, small and large, nourished by their connection with the heart; the signs are as vital as when they were made, carved, built, painted; the works of their art as powerful as when they were new.

One day, we used to say, as we made our small journeys in the middle of France, we will follow these routes to their end. We will go to Compostela. So here we are, about to set forth. Cosmo and me, without children this time, in a small red car and full of expectancy; we travel well together, we've been doing it for a long time.

You might think this is an historic kind of thing to

do, archaic, a backward-looking act of piety more architectural than religious, in my case. Not so. We are travelling the pilgrim route as people always have, for our own reasons. Nor are there any less of us now than ever there were.

In the Middle Ages pilgrims mostly went on foot; the rich travelled on horseback but the poor always walked. There were even professional beggars who made a life's work out of travelling the pilgrim routes. Such journeys imply peace and order; when the Turks invade the Holy Land you choose somewhere safer. At first the intrepid must brave brigands and greedy innkeepers and cheats and touts of every ingenious kind, but gradually the journey becomes safer. It's marked in stages, so that each evening you can be sure of shelter from snow, wolves, bandits. This is never perfect, of course; there will always be dishonest hoteliers who'll empty out your stores of water while you sleep, in order to sell you bad wine at an exorbitant price. But almost from the beginning there are guidebooks warning of pitfalls, recommending good accommodation, telling you what to expect; the first, the *Codex Calixtinus*, written in Latin, followed by English, Italian, French, German texts. All offering detailed itineraries of painless pilgrimages.

Pilgrims were tourists from the start. Pilgrims invented tourism. And in return all tourists are pilgrims, in their way. All looking for something, some meaning, some knowledge, some experience, they'll recognise when they find it. The old tourism of pilgrimages offers useful new pilgrimages of tourism, and so the world turns and endlessly contemplates itself.

These days you get signs on all the roads, none too major or too minor to flash the cockle-shell that tells you that you are travelling a route to Compostela. But the serious pilgrim still goes on foot. Or possibly on a bicycle. Sometimes taking a television crew to record the journey, the perils and the characters met on the way. You don't have to do it all in one go. Some people spend three years of summer holidays completing it in stages. Others walk only parts of it. I've got an up-to-the-minute book of the path from Cahors to Roncevaux: '1.5 km, 30 min, Pech de la Rode; 3.5 km, 50 min, Lauzerte; 3 km, 45 min, Eglise de St Cernin', and so on, page after page, with geography and history and small symbols indicating where food is to be had, and shopping, camping, hotels, trains. With little pieces of advice: 'It's interesting to make this trip in the spring, for the fruit trees which line the slopes and the open country of the Garonne offer magnificent colours and give out an agreeable perfume.'

The routes are not main roads, they are special pedestrian paths, signposted, maintained; they've been in use since the twelfth century and earlier. You are treading in ancient footsteps when you take these paths.

You should walk, for the contemplation of it, the time to think that's hard to find in daily life. Walking is mind-clearing, body-testing; in the more than two months it will take you to get to Compostela the old body dies, a new one is born. So say the walkers. We're driving; we're greedy and want to see a lot of places. We do not have this single-minded pedestrian leisure.

Note beside the cockle-shell the flag of Europe, this new entity Europe, not flying but painted on signs all along the highways: a circle of gold stars on a blue field. A kind of *campus stellae*.

PILGRIMS

The dress of a medieval pilgrim: thick-soled shoes, to deal with paths paved with flints and thorns; a wide-brimmed hat for shelter from rain and sun; a cape thick enough to protect from cold and short enough not to catch on brambles; a water-bottle in some unbreakable material; a wallet fastened round the waist by a belt (to pay if need be for lodgings, and to receive alms); a scrip or over-the-shoulder bag for bread and any baggage; a staff, heavy and crooked at the end, to serve as a cane and also as a weapon. The only decoration, but much more than adornment, being a sign and symbol of the pilgrim's state, a cockle-shell. Worn perhaps on a string round the neck, or sewn in the hat, it shows he has been, or means to go, to Santiago de Compostela in Galicia, where such shells are common on the beaches.

This is the figure that Sir Walter Raleigh is describing in the poem 'His Pilgrimage':

Give me my scallop-shell of quiet,
  My staff of faith to walk upon,

> *My scrip of joy, immortal diet,*
> > *My bottle of salvation,*
> *My gown of glory, hope's true gage,*
> > *And thus I'll take my pilgrimage.*

Life is a pilgrimage; the journey from the cradle to the grave easily turns into such a metaphor. Or the allegory of Bunyan's *The Pilgrim's Progress*, in which Christian, carrying a burden on his back, must leave the City of Destruction and try to make his way to the Celestial City, avoiding such pitfalls as the Slough of Despond, the Valley of Humiliation, Doubting Castle, the Delectable Mountains. His friend Faithful is killed in Vanity Fair, but Christian wins through. Just as well there's some kind of happy ending, under the circumstances. The full title of the book is *The Pilgrim's Progress from this world to that which is to come delivered under the similitude of a dream*.

The dress of a modern pilgrim: thick-soled shoes, hiking boots or some brand-named running shoes, hat, cape, water-bottle, wallet on a belt (known as a bum bag in some circles), scrip, staff and cockle-shells. At Puente la Reina, the small town in Spain where all the roads converge, the ancient pilgrim hospice is swarming with people this summer Sunday; a lunch is being held. Suddenly the crowds part. Two figures come striding in, scallop-shells clanking. Dressed exactly as above, plus dark glasses. And shorts and teeshirts. How stout they are, how full of importance. All the ancient holy weight of centuries mantles them along with their cloaks. The rest of us are spectators. Not worth a glance.

Later we see the two men in the car park, standing at the boot of a shining new red station-wagon, loading all the gear, the staffs and scrips and hats and cloaks, into it. Heigh-ho. Each must make his own pilgrimage, her own pilgrimage, as seems to them best.

PILGRIMAGE

A pilgrimage is a tracing and a retracing of a journey. It is always, in a sense, a going again, even if it is your first time, because you travel in the consciousness of the people who've gone before you. A pilgrimage is made to a place where something has already happened, but where the happening is not sealed in the past; you go because it is a place where something may still happen today for you. Even if it is just — hardly just! — finding out about yourself.

THE JOURNEY BEGINS

Plane journeys. The brief one from the high country to the city by the sea. Sydney the city of water. As you fly in from Canberra, over the Blue Mountains then down across the plains you see that there is almost as much water as land, it shines like metal set in curious shapes and polished. You arrive to queue for the giant craft in which you are packed, scientifically maybe, but without care. You recognise your own insignificance in this overcrowded space. Who would have thought so many people could afford to pay so much money to be so uncomfortable.

Sydney to Hong Kong: looking out the window at apartment buildings at the wing tips. So far the plane must always have missed them. More waiting. Hong Kong to Paris. This stage will take fourteen hours instead of twelve, we have to make a detour because of trouble in the Middle East. That's how people came to go to Compostela in the first place: trouble in the Middle East.

PARIS

We must go and look at the church of the pilgrims. The church where they used to start, near the present rue de Rivoli, was enormous, you can see from the size of the park which along with its tower is all that remains. People would hear mass there and then set off; there was a milestone at the base of the tower with zero written on it. But the next church has survived; it's called St James, too, of the High Step; St Jacques du Haut Pas. Named after an order of friars, *les frères hospitaliers* of St Jacques d'Altopascio from Tuscany; they looked after the poor and the sick, and welcomed pilgrims. The thirteenth-century king of France known as St Louis founded the order of these friars in Paris; their hospital constituted the first link in a chain of hospitals on the Paris–Compostela route. A pleasant enough parish church, with children's paintings pinned up and notices about the first communion picnic at the weekend, a church busy living in the present, though in one corner is a series of posters giving its history, and here the pilgrims are mentioned. It has been freshly cleaned of centuries of grime, so is wonderfully clear and light, of pale stone, with only a little coloured glass and that not rich, with round arches and Corinthian pilasters; a seventeenth-century church, can't hold a candle to Romanesque, with a chill to it rather welcome on this hot day, were it not of an ecclesiastical stuffiness that you might think was the odour of sanctity. The inhabitants of the quarter built it, it was a poor area, they had no money, so they gave one day's work a week free.

RUE ST JACQUES

The name of the street is also St James: the rue St Jacques. It's a long street which runs from the boulevard du Port Royal right at the top of the Luxembourg Gardens down to the Seine; you can stand by the quays and watch it rise in a long gully where the traffic flows like a river going the wrong way between banks of intricate grey architecture. Before Lutece was occupied by the Romans — Lutece was the city on the Seine before it was named Paris — the rue St Jacques was a busy road for travellers across Gaul.

I have two reasons for being interested in this street. One is that I lived here, for a month in the winter of 1989, in an apartment like a motel room, with a comfortable bed and a fat silvery-blue lounge suite. The space was plushy and hot and dull, except when you put red tulips in a vase, and then it cheered up. It had a little dining table with two chairs. When friends came to dine they had to bring their own. One couple walked through the Latin Quarter carrying little cane stools that looked like drums, as though they were going to play in a band. The kitchen wasn't the worst of the hell holes I have known, though you couldn't fit two people in it at the same time; one had to come out to make room for the other. The bathroom was much bigger and fitted out in brownish mauve marble. We supposed that you bathed and scented and painted yourself and went out for meals.

I loved that apartment. I'd sit in the window and gaze at the view of an eighteenth-century gateway and beside it a narrow strip of the Val de Grâce, a vast domed seventeenth-century church built by a queen of France called Anne of Austria in gratitude and also keeping a promise, the bargain she'd made with God: give me a son and I'll give you a church. She got Louis XIV and God got the Val de Grâce.

Opposite was a shop called Danuta selling children's clothes. Its windows glowed with brightly coloured tiny garments, many of them red, lit with yellow lights and the façade decorated with boughs of evergreen. A lot of shops hang themselves with greenery at Christmas. And I'd look at this little shop, the grey stone, the cold grey air, these bright little garments, garlanded in the mysterious dark foliage of evergreen boughs, and I had then and still have a sense of it as marvellous, as a perfect bright image of Christmas. Part of the marvel being that these quite simple elements should achieve such power. They were after all just expensive clothes for rich babies; you'd gasp at the price. But evergreens are mythical, they belong to ceremonies long before Christianity, they affirm greenness and growing in days of cold and no sun, they deck this grey stone harsh as winter with their own stubborn aliveness, even while they perish. And when you stand beside them you can smell the sap, even when it no longer flows, becoming more pungent as it dies and dries.

ROLAND BARTHES

The other thing I always think of when I am in the rue St Jacques is the death of Roland Barthes. In this street, at the corner where the rue des Ecoles crosses it, happened the motor accident that killed him. I've heard it said that he was run over by a laundry van, as though there's something in that a bit ludicrous, which thus makes it more tragic, and the waste worse. I think a more terrible irony is that it happened here, right beside the Sorbonne; he was at home here, in these streets, he walked this area all his life, you would not expect a violent death in so familiar a place.

One of the things I like about Barthes is the connection he made between language and gastronomy. Between food and words. They both have the same organ, the tongue: it is the tongue that speaks, and the tongue that tastes. Without the tongue all this orality is lost (and so is kissing).

We're back to food and stories, again.

I also like his idea of literature, that it is the awareness language has of being language. It's not an instrument to convey a meaning, an idea, a fact, a truth: what it means is itself. It is the thought, it's not about the thought. The thought forms itself in the mouth. As though you can taste it as your tongue speaks it.

Barthes' passionate belief was that anything the human mind might light upon is fit matter for this process: wrestling, or Citroens, steak and chips, the recipes in *Elle* magazine, soap powder, striptease, Garbo's face.

So, what counts is not the subject, but the way language invents itself in the presence of this subject. What it is becomes what you do with it. That's my interpretation, anyway. As a novelist I'm pleased to hear it. I never met Barthes, never sat at his feet as did many of his acolytes, never even went to one of his Sorbonne lectures, but whenever I walk along the rue St Jacques I take particular thought before I step off the footpaths.

ASPARAGUS

As a kind of preparation for our pilgrimage we stay a couple of days with Bernard and Grant in their house a little way from Paris, they've recently chosen this country living, in the Ile de France. The countryside is famous for its bocage, Bernard says that's why they bought the house here: the small woods, the copses, like the poetic English word bosky, and indeed I discover that in the dictionary there is an ancient word boscage, which means wooded scenery. Cosmo recalls Ronsard writing poems about the bocage being destroyed, this was in the sixteenth century, but it seems to be surviving, the woods are flourishing in their early summer green. The soil is fertile, crumbly grey, with small cultivated fields. This countryside is called the garden of France, for its flowers and in a vegetable sense. Bernard's other requirement for country living was a bakery and paper-shop; they're around the corner, about ninety seconds' walk away. A minute or so the other way along leafy paths is the river.

We buy some asparagus, at a shop Grant tells us is expensive but always good, and take it home and work out how to cook it. It's the white kind. I'm used to the green, with the white coming only in tins, though the closing of the Edgell's canning factory is supposed to have made a little of the white available. The spears are large and glistening and fat; it's asparagus out of a painting. We peel it, and cook it in a little water until it is tender, and serve it with a vinaigrette: it's sublime. It has that sweet, nutty, slightly unearthly taste of certain vegetables that grow in the earth; whereas the green is sharp and fresh and grassy, as are things that grow upon it. The white is probably more marvellous, but less trustworthy; the spears may be fibrous and fit more for sucking on than chewing up. The green is more dependable.

The next day we have lunch at La Tour de Cheroy, in the village of that name; it used to be La Tour d'Argent until Claude Terrail of the Paris three-star restaurant claimed the name and everybody else had to give it up, even those who'd had it longer. A real French lunch in the country: terrines, *rillettes de saumon, asperges blanches* — more of the marvellous fat white spears, tender to the very end of the stalk, mild, sweet. *Blanquette de veau. Steack maître d'hôtel.* Simple, a bit rustic. *Fromage frais* and *sorbets.*

Afterwards we go for a walk by their river, a small lively stream in narrow channels and wide, flowing across weirs and through locks and down steps and over mill races, turning up in surprising places. And all along its edge private *lavoirs*, small huts really with ancient tiled roofs, sometimes filled with junk, old timber, lumber, sometimes decorated with tubs of flowers. And a public one, newly restored, though nobody uses any of them for washing any more. When I first went to Sévérac women still used the public *lavoir* at the end of the street, but only for washing their husbands' work clothes; there'd be a group of them and lots of laughing and talking.

Great weighty stems of roses everywhere, even growing out of a tiny square of gravel beside a stone cottage wall.

EN ROUTE

First day out of Paris. Lunch in Nevers, at
l'Aquarella. A big café-restaurant. Entirely typical,
with its terrace, its separate spaces, its rooms
upstairs. To eat: a *salade du marché* — *du supermarché*
more like. Asparagus out of a tin, when not fifty
kilometres from here and two days ago we had such
fresh asparagus as needed a chapter to itself, and
beans tinned too, sweet corn ditto. The French fondness for industrial sweet corn is mysterious. I eat
andouillette which translates as tripe sausage; little
pink furls and knots and nubbles of gristle, spicy,
herby, very slightly urinatious and its absolute deliciousness quite possibly, at least in part, relief that
it is not more so. I like dangerous food, that balances
delicately on the knife's edge or even the fork's
point: how easily it could all go wrong. Indeed for
some people it already has. They wouldn't eat tripe
sausage to save their lives. I always eat *andouillette*
first thing in France, I haven't arrived till I've had
one. I've never found any in this country; we're
good copycats of such a variety of sausage products
I wonder why this one has escaped us. I keep looking, and thought I had some tracked down to
Jonathan's in Fitzroy, in Melbourne, but they don't
make them very often, about twice a year in fact, so
I can't report.

The chips are excellent. With this some Pouilly
Fumé from just up the road.

The cathedral has new stained glass which is
spectacular and doesn't fill you with despair that we

should be such poor imitators of the first masters of these buildings. The artists are very famous and have not tried to be traditional. We call in at Moulins to have another look at the great triptych but there's a funeral on, a very grand one, so sight-seeing is off. We try again on the way back but it's Sunday and the cathedral's shut all morning for Mass, so we miss it again.

CALENDAR

On to Souvigny. Bernard mentioned that there's a font here into which women who wanted to get pregnant stuck their heads, but I can't find it. Nor anybody I'm prepared to ask. There are some tombs, and a statue of St Mayeul, and a fine cloister. Across the way is another church, more ancient, which for a while was used as a garage. Now it's a museum, *un musée lapidaire* which means it has a lot of worked stone, capitals, altars, ancient sarcophagi, and a twelfth-century calendar, an octagonal pillar carved with the works of the months: September treading grapes, October feeding acorns to pigs; it makes us think of our acorns at home, millions of them, all as we speak ambitious to turn themselves into oak trees. On other sides are the corresponding signs of the zodiac, fabulous beasts, and finally symbols of mysterious people. It has the simple rightness and power of so much Romanesque carving; the pig, the man, the shapely leaves of the oak tree carved with an innocent yet comprehending eye.

Now is June. The weather is hot, hot. It's Monday, the café's shut. Just up the road is a one-star hotel. At Bourbon l'Archambault. Fourteen kilometres away on a small road winding through summer fields and hedgerows.

BEDS

We arrive sweaty and grubby and our hair full of wind, through having to drive with the windows open. We park the car, step on to the terrace, are met by *monsieur*. The *maître d'hôtel*, quite literally, and possibly the proprietor. He decides we don't want to spend an extravagant amount of money, and makes appropriate suggestions. Shows us to a large room, with two big iron beds, and mattresses in the old style, that can be redone, remade. That is, they have no springs, they are made of wool that can be shaken up, sort of aerated, and rebuttoned. They're firm, hard enough, but excellent to sleep on. A good mattress in the hands of a thrifty housewife can keep going a long time. She doesn't do it herself, there's a tradesman for such a job. Occasionally you see a faded sign on an old shopfront: *Matelassier*. It's one of those crafts that have nearly died out. You don't preserve, you discard. Or in some places, keep but neglect, in which case they're like sleeping on a lumpy mountain side. If you doze off at all you wake exhausted with the effort of not rolling off.

The beds are traditional but the shower isn't. It's so high tech I can't work out how to turn it on, Cosmo has to do it.

Clean, we sit in the garden, where a maid is sweeping gravel out of the flowerbeds. There is shade from thickly leaved lime trees, but it is still warm, the heat-exhausted end of a summer's day, when the air is as enervated as you are. Some cold white wine is needed. They don't sell it by the glass, but we can begin the dinner bottle. A St Pourcain, a fresh dry white from just down the road. With a little plate of savoury *friandises* each and the menu to study.

THE WATERS

Some old people come creeping out for a little wander or sit, well wrapped up in case of evening chill. These are the long-term visitors, *en pension*, they have their own dining-room, and now though not quite eight o'clock is after dinner. They are here to take the waters, for this is a spa town, famous since Roman times. The water that gushes forth at fifty-five degrees Celsius, full of minerals like magnesium, potassium, lithium, rare gases like helium, neon, krypton, and with a mild radioactivity, is good for all sorts of rheumatisms, both inflammatory and degenerative, for neuralgias, paralyses, and even gynaecological problems. The town's name evokes both the Gallic god Borvo, protector of thermal springs, and the first lords of Bourbon, the Archambaults. Numbers of famous people have been clients, like Talleyrand who came every summer for thirty years to bathe. The locals joined him in all sorts of pleasure parties. There were games of whist, and gossip with his barber, Latin jokes with his doctor, conversation. It was because of these healing summers that he kept on top of the tricky pile of early nineteenth-century European politics for so much longer than any of his contemporaries could manage; so it was said.

All this I found out later, reading the guidebook. I wish I could spend a fortnight here. I reckon a good course of *hydrokinébalnéothérapie thermale* would set me up wonderfully.

À LA CARTE

At this moment it's food we have in mind. We decide not to take any of the set-price menus but to dine *à la carte*, to eat delicately rather than lavishly. Not taking a menu gives you the freedom not to eat …

To begin with, we share a dish of *Foie gras maison* with hot toasts. *Maison* means that they cook the whole liver on the premises, in house, so it's fresh, not preserved in tins, or half-preserved so it keeps for a while. Both these ways of preparing goose liver, or duck liver, are good, but they can't compare with the new fresh product. I read somewhere recently that someone in Australia is experimenting with fattening livers in this manner. I hope they'll succeed; it's a sublime dish. Sydney Smith said his idea of heaven was *foie gras* to the sound of trumpets. The part of this I am not sure about is the trumpets. I love trumpet music, but in this context I think they might be a bit brassy and braying. What about organs instead? There you've got marvellous noise, great power and volume if you want it, but also an ethereal sweetness which is much more what *foie gras* is about. Or perhaps a choir ... singing Handel's *Ode for St Cecilia's Day*. Or Kiri Te Kanawa and songs of the Auvergne. That's geographically appropriate; we're on the edge of the Auvergne here, in the region called the Bourbonnais; it's the *Michelin* green guide for this area that told me about Talleyrand and the Gallic god. But perhaps the songs are too full of yearning, and that is not appropriate. I like music that is yearning, and that may be a kind of heavenly striving, but the thing about heaven is that the striving, for goodness, or love, or some perfect spirit, the striving is over, you have it. So perhaps the point about trumpets is that they don't yearn, they affirm, and Sydney Smith is right.

And anyway *foie gras* in the smooth knife-tinkling silence of a restaurant is already heavenly. While you are eating it, you are free of desire, for it is being fulfilled.

RECIPE FOR *FOIE GRAS* IN AUSTRALIA

Go to a reputable shop and buy the best they have. Read the label very carefully; the ingredients should consist of nothing but *foie gras*, with possibly a little truffle, and some wine, like champagne, or Sauternes. If it mentions pork put it back. You don't need a big quantity; you eat just a little, slowly and delectably. Serve with some fine hot white bread toasts. It will cost quite a lot of money, but less than eating in a restaurant.

A LA CARTE CONTINUED

Next we have a crown of *langoustines* and *coquilles St-Jacques* (we haven't entirely forgotten about Compostela) with a purée of leeks and some morels. The dishes come with a flourish: a silver underplate each, the food on a porcelain plate, with a silver dome over; the waiter puts them down and removes the domes simultaneously. This is the waiterly theatre that *haute cuisine* carried to such a dramatic art.

There are no shells on the seafood, the flesh forms a ring around a little mound of leeks: this is the crown. The *langoustines* are tiny sweet morsels of shellfish, the corals on the scallops big and brightly coloured.

Cosmo finishes with a *petit pot de crème caramel avec ses sables*; *sable* means sand, but of course it's the lightness and crispness of these little biscuits that is meant. We've had the dining-room to ourselves almost since we arrived, but nobody is hurrying us. This is a meal of grace and leisure, its calmness, its ceremony the perfect restorative after a day's travelling.

'WHILE WORTH VISITING'

Afterwards we go for a walk through the town. The scent of the lime blossom is heavy and dry honey sweet in the summer night. Though here in France people will say it isn't summer till the solstice, 21 June, but this seems to me too close to midsummer, which is 24 June, St John the Baptist's day. St James' day is a month later. The nomenclature hardly matters; this feels like summer, the scent of the lime flowers could make you think of Proust, and underneath is a whiff of drains, and of *mazout*. I like this smell of old cities; it reminds you that civilisation is hardly won. There are silver domes on the dishes and small rose-coloured shades on the table lamps, the limes are planted in fragrant rows to cool the hot days, but underneath are the everlasting drains. The fallible drains.

The town is deserted, but well lit. We can peer up at the massive ruined towers of the castle. One of them is called la tour Quiquengrogne, a name which means 'let them complain'. The town seems to have grown up through the castle like weeds through paving.

When we get back to the hotel the beds are turned down and the shutters closed. We've got a quiet room, at the back; as though the front were at all noisy, in this sleepy early-to-bed town.

We have breakfast at the same table as dinner: hot jugs of coffee and milk, croissants, bread, a cone of frothy butter, warm fruity brioche. On the way down we passed the dining-room for the guests *en pension*, empty and frugal, with its re-corked bottles of wine and water, hardly touched. When we pay the bill the *maître d'hôtel* finally asks us our names. So far we have been guests and host, the idea of payment never discussed. Certainly no impression of credit card taken. I have admired his superb professional uncuriosity that protects our privacy and saves him the effort of making our acquaintance. Though when it is apparent we are Australian — our Visa cards are such a gaudy red that they always surprise, compared to the cool blue of European banks, as though we're handing out toy money, and so we get into conversations about that — he tells us he has two sons there. But he doesn't expect ever to visit, his wife is not well enough to travel. And you can see he doesn't want to; the perfect orderliness of his hotel is what pleases him.

We call in at le Grand Etablissement Thermal, a most grandiose building exactly opposite the hotel, which is called l'Hôtel Thermes. People walk to and from it in their dressing-gowns. Very valetudinarian this looks. The building is arched and balustraded inside, with marvellous tile murals, watery ones of birds and plants, gold and turquoise peacock feather patterns, and on the grand staircase a picture of 'the allegorical goddess of the waters of Bourbon l'Archambault'. The air is hot, full of steam. The place is like a hospital: desks, nurses, waiting-rooms, patients, a serious atmosphere. What about Talleyrand and his pleasure parties? You can take the waters on the national health, if you've got medical reasons, like re-education after a stroke, or osteoarthritis, or hypofunctioning of the ovaries.

As well as the hot springs this area has the most significant concentration of Romanesque churches to be found in France. As my pamphlet says, translating a little of itself into a kind of English: 'Bourbon is a historic town and a reknown spa ... Bourbon is while worth visiting.'

Nearby is the hamlet of Ygrande, which has a twelfth-century church with one of the finest stone spires in the region. A spire is Romanesque architecture finally giving up any regard for classical architecture. The round-arched solid-to-the-ground sheltering space is no longer content just to enclose. It aspires upwards. You could say that a spire points to a new optimism after an ungrateful millennium; somebody did, I think — I wrote it down, but not the name of the author. A thousand years after the beginning of Christianity, and people suddenly find the right architecture for it. Which almost immediately reaches its apotheosis, before the long and glorious decline of the Gothic.

Just before Ygrande a sign points down a tiny rough road to St Plaisir. St Pleasure. Who is St Plaisir? How can we find out? He might be good to choose as a patron saint.

THE FOOD OF EUROPE

All over France and I presume all over the Common Market countries are roads marked E for Europe. Where French roads have tended to go up and down the map, that is, north and south, those with an E are more generally horizontal, going to Spain, coming from Poland, Romania, who knows. They are the ungrateful heirs of the great transcontinental pilgrim routes. These roads are to be avoided on all counts. For one thing, they are not as good as they ought to be. They're not motorways, or autoroutes; they mostly have four lanes but you can't depend on it, they shrink suddenly, they are prone to roadworks, either building them or rebuilding them as they crumble under the terrible weight and volume of the traffic that roars along them. Of course, this is largely trucks, that's what the roads are for, to get truckloads of goods from one side of the Union to the other, never mind that each has its own products, it's communality we're talking here. And if you shift wine lakes and butter mountains from place to place people might not notice they exist.

The noise is something Dante could have made good use of, for one of his circles of hell. When you're in a small red car, on a hot day, with no air-conditioning so you have to have the windows down, with enormous screaming trucks in front, behind, on either side, and the sense you're not driving fast enough for any of them, hell is where you think you are.

The E roads have their own food. Chips. Up and down their verges are *friteries* selling *frites*. These *friteries* are shacks, tents, rickety caravans, usually painted blue, a colour with excellent fading qualities, and parked by the road, in lay-bys, in fields. *FRITES*, you'll see a sign, usually home-made, which the chips probably aren't, and shortly afterwards the *friterie* will appear. Often abandoned. And even when functioning, hardly flourishing. Most of them studies in the forlorn, even when there's a car or two of patrons.

I'm a devotee of chips. I agree with Barthes on the quintessential Frenchness of them. He calls them 'the alimentary sign of Frenchness'. Sign being one of the more important words in Barthes' vocabulary. But his chips are associated with steak: it is steak that 'communicates its national glamour to them: chips are nostalgic and patriotic like steak'.

But the forlorn chip vans were not offering steak. I think it's possible that they were Belgian, rather than French. I've seen such vehicles there; one I remember in Bruges, which seemed to have a permanent place in a small square. One evening I saw it pouring a drum of used cooking oil — gallons of it, tens of litres — down a hole in the gutter. I like to think this was an inlet especially for the disposal of oils and greases, that maybe there's a network of noxious waste pipes serving the whole city, but I fear not. The French tell jokes about the Belgians, as do the English about the Irish and the Canadians about Newfoundlanders and Danes about the people of Greenland, though political correctness is trying to put a stop to them. But there are things to be learned from racist jokes. This one is best spoken, with actions. Its central image is of people with open paper cornets of chips, though you could picture paper bags or even small cardboard buckets held in the left hand.

Question: Why is the central place of Brussels littered with chips every day at noon?

Answer: Because that's when the great clock strikes midday and all the Belgians eating their lunch in the square look at their watches to see if it's right. (You make an elaborate gesture of turning your left arm to look at your watch.)

Chips everywhere.

Maybe there was some Belgian plot to cover the E roads of Europe with chips from handy *frites* vans. If so, it seems to have foundered, in France at any rate. I suppose in the interests of research I should have tried some, they might have been the most delicious chips in the world, thin, crisp, sizzling hot, sinfully salted. But the little red car never found the moment or the courage to make its escape from its screaming escort of trucks, and on more gentle and leisurely roads the vans hadn't cared to set up shop.

THE FAILURE OF THE PICNIC

The E roads are so tiring that we avoid them wherever possible and take quieter more wandering ways. Here fat green trees cool the eye if not the air, and there is rarely another car to be seen. By the second night out from Paris we are in Rocamadour.

Lunch we had at La Souterraine. We keep meaning to have picnics, but this isn't easy. If you leave it too late the shops are all shut in these sleepy towns and anyway it's so much simpler to pop into a restaurant. We found one in a hotel called La Porte St Jean, actually built under the medieval gate which was part of the fortifications of the old city. Here the menu was forty-eight francs (about twelve Australian dollars) including a pitcher of okay light wine. We get the *plat du jour*, roast shoulder of veal with a *sauce provençale* (*provençale* being as glamorous and misused a word in France as in Australia), here a pleasant tomato sauce, with waxy steamed potatoes. Followed by cheese which turns out to be a salad with cubes of fresh cheese and another very like a Milawa washed rind which the woman serving doesn't know the name of. Although we've come in and sat down at about one o'clock we're alone, though there's evidence that the café part where we're sitting has had a full complement of customers already eaten and left, and in the grander restaurant there are still people lunching more lengthily. I think it might be bosses in there, workers out here.

MOZARABIC

The church is one of those which starts off Romanesque but turns out Gothic, because of taking several centuries to build. The shape and carving of the portal at the western end is mozarabic in style which is probably owing to pilgrims from Compostela. Mozarabs being Christians in Muslim

Spain who were allowed to practise their religion, provided they paid their allegiance to the Moorish king. A kind of rendering unto Caesar that Christ would have approved of. The Moors were broad-minded and generous, they allowed both Christians and Jews to keep their own religions. Unlike the Christians after the Reconquest, who did their best to stamp everybody else out. Greedily wanting religious as well as temporal power. It took them centuries of fighting to get rid of the Moors, and by that time they were so much in the habit that they turned their crusading zeal against their own people by inventing the Inquisition.

A Moorish-Romanesque style turns up in odd corners in Europe, and it's always very moving. I remember getting off a boat in Messina, in Sicily, a passenger liner which docked hours later than scheduled, only for a few hours, and peering in the dark of nearly midnight at a small church with round arches in Muslim patterns. And there's the marvellous tympanum at Conques: inscribed on the robe of an angel are some words in Arabic, in Cufic script. *Al-houm*, it says, which means happiness.

GUIDES

How do you find your way around France? It's easy. You use a guidebook. Whenever I am in this part of the world I think of Gerard Manley Hopkins' line: 'Generations have trod, have trod, have trod ... ' In France the treading of those generations, those of the past and those yet to come, are thoroughly mapped in guidebooks.

THE RED GUIDE

So, you buy a guidebook. Possibly several. But not too many, or you will get confused. I have given my allegiance to Michelin. If I am planning to travel about the country, the first thing I do when I arrive is buy the red *Guide Michelin*, the one with hotels and restaurants, graded according to comfort and quality in various categories. Food follows the famous, and possibly infamous, star system:

*** *Exceptional cuisine, worth a special journey*
   Superb food, fine wines, faultless service, elegant surroundings. One will pay accordingly!

 ** *Excellent cooking, worth a detour*
   Specialities and wines of first-class quality. This will be reflected in the price.

  * *A very good restaurant in its category*
   The star indicates a good place to stop on your journey. But beware of comparing the star given to an expensive de luxe establishment to that of a simple restaurant where you can appreciate fine cuisine at a reasonable price.

Already there's some subtlety involved; the guide will advise but not think for you.

You'll notice that the three-star rating mentions elegant surroundings: this means crystal glassware, porcelain plates, fine linen, it takes into account the carpets and curtains, or whatever fills their role; in other words a high standard of luxury must apply to everything, not just the cooking. Sometimes chefs say that it's the classiness of the toilets that gets them their third star, not the quality of the food. It's certainly pleasant to have piles of small soft towels instead of a hot-air machine, and a cake of soap, and lights that flatter rather than an interrogational strip of fluorescence.

On the other hand, sometimes you may not feel like such grandeur. Or such rich food. You want to eat well, but in more modest surroundings. The *Michelin* gives what I call a *Repas rouge*, that is, it writes *Repas* in red beside restaurants with 'less elaborate, moderately priced menus that offer good value for money and serve carefully prepared meals, often of regional cooking'. You might manage four or five such meals for the price of a three star. I've plotted whole itineraries around *Repas rouges*, often staying at them since they are usually hotels, old-fashioned family places following a strict and orderly tradition. Here is bourgeois virtue at its busy best.

The *Michelin* rates its hotels too, from luxury to simple comfort, the symbol for the last being a wineglass and fork with a roof over. There are red brackets for attractive features, red arrows for views, green seats for gardens, a bird for quietness, which will be red if it's very quiet, as well as symbols for gyms, dogs, parking, television, lifts, tennis, to name just a few, so that altogether you can spend hours balancing the merits of peace, scenery, sports, and medieval beams. Plus price of course, and whether you want to stop in this particular place anyway, or keep driving to the next.

Somehow the *Michelin* seems less useful in Paris, perhaps because there are so many more establishments than it can include. Its most modest tend to be expensive. And anyway one of the best things about taking walks round Paris is reading the menus outside restaurants and peering in the windows and imagining eating in them. You can get a pretty good idea. As in Australia, the menu prose gives good advance warning of what to expect. Though in Paris fashion is less of an element. But flowery prose is always bad news.

THE GREEN GUIDE

Michelin also does green guides, to the countryside, its geographical and architectural beauties, its history and legends. These are marvellous for looking at churches and castles and beginning to understand the things you are seeing. I wouldn't have come across the ubiquitous story of the fattened pig and the lifting of the siege had I not read it again and again in the green guide.

There are other brands than Michelin. Kleber is one, and a lot of people like the relative newcomer Gault & Millau, which gives chef's hats instead of stars to mark its restaurants. They rarely agree, which makes choice difficult if you are using both. This is why you need a navigator as you're driving round, not so much to find your way on the map as to correlate the guides.

I mention brands of guidebook because of course that's what they are, large commercial enterprises, and in the case of Michelin and Kleber linked to even bigger business: the manufacture of tyres. Which is no accident. Travellers' guides in the twentieth century are a creation of the motor industry.

CURNONSKY

It would help in talking about this if the name Curnonsky were familiar but this is unlikely. He was not a creator of recipes like Escoffier or Carème, and thus not apt for reissuing in a glossy new cookbook to please collectors, who owning all the new ones have to raid the past. Curnonsky was a writer about food, a philosopher, a critic, an arbiter, a describer, a daily ephemeral journalist.

He was born in the Anjou region in 1872, of a mother who died giving birth to him, and brought up by a cultivated and lively grandmother who wasn't married to his grandfather, in a house where a devoted servant, a widow, made marvellous meals for forty years; she cooked, he said, as a bird sings. His name wasn't Curnonsky then, it was Maurice Edmond Sailland.

At twenty he went to Paris to study at the Sorbonne, taking grandma and the cook to look after him. But quickly he fell into the company of wits, men of letters, men about town: writers, poets, journalists. In those days a witty remark would make you famous, not just in their company but in the literary world, the world of readers. He was charmed by *la vie de bohème*; this bohemian life seemed much more attractive than the life of the university and the Latin Quarter.

From the moment his first Paris friend took him to a little restaurant called la Côte d'Or, in the rue Racine, where Perroud was patron and his wife and daughters ran the place, serving family food, *pot au feu*, roast chicken, fillet of veal, good cheeses, a decent little Auxerre wine, with Chambertin on feast days, and he discovered the marvellous company to be kept there, the Sorbonne didn't have a chance. Teachers and grandmother remonstrated. Useless. The young man was already embarked on the life which would see him living in an apartment without a dining-room, which for sixty years would know him as a man about town, living by fork and pen. A multi-pronged pen it was too. Grandma and the cook returned to Anjou.

Sailland's youth and cleverness seduced the literary crowd; they adopted him. He discovered he could write for journals and get paid for it. One day a friend said that Maurice Sailland was a hopeless name for one of his profession; he needed a pen name. *Nom de guerre*, he called it. He suggested something Russian: the tsar was visiting Paris, Stravinsky was on all the posters, Russian was fashionable. What about something ending in -sky?

Sailland had been a Latin scholar. Whynotsky, he replied, only in Latin: Curnonsky. And so he became. His friends played around, added Boris and Bogislas to it, called him Prince. Sailland himself came to regret it; he was arrested as a spy, and almost didn't get the *Légion d'honneur* on the grounds that he was a foreigner. He whose family had lived in Anjou for fifteen generations. He once described his name as his 'shirt of Nessus', the poisoned shirt with which Hercules' wife unwittingly killed her husband. Sailland didn't have a wife. He dined with women, but that was as close as he seemed to get to them.

COLETTE

So, Curnonsky is in Paris, at *la fin de siècle*. Among the people he meets is Colette, who is married at this time to Willy. Both Colette and Curnonsky write novels for Willy. Willy's name is a pseudonym too; he is Gauthier-Villars who publishes light and frothy novels and is always on the lookout for a hired pen. Colette and Curnonsky are Willy's *nègres*, which means ghost writers; Willy publishes them under his own name. Some of the titles of Curnonsky's books are: *Lelie Opium Smoker*; *Beach of Love*; *Suzette Wants to Leave Me in the Lurch*; *The Implacable Syska*. Willy is a hard master; he gets angry if the writing isn't done fast enough.

Colette of course goes on to become one of the great novelists of the twentieth century. On the occasion of Curnonsky's birthday, in 1952, when they were both eighty, she wrote to him, asking did he remember those early days when:

> ... you were a nice boy of 21 with a sweet face; I was a cold unsociable girl whose provincial origins could be read in her features, her silence, her long plaits, her dresses which were straight out of her village ... from afar you watched me getting married here and there, while you raised culinary art to its noble level as a French art. So that today, of the two of us, it is you who are the most provincial, the most crunchy, the most golden-browned. Clairvoyance and gourmandise are upon you, those lucid and good smelling things, and you sing of them in a language in which I taste at once your modesty and perfect assurance.

On the radio, for the same birthday, she said, 'Cur and I were the two main contributors to the Willy workshops. We never worked together. But we worked bloody hard for mister Willy.'

Well, Colette's fame flourishes, it grows from generation to generation, but Curnonsky's seems to have died with him. At least in French popular memory. I can find no mention of him in the *Robert* or the *Larousse Dictionaries of Proper Names*, under either of his. There were a lot of dishes named after him, in the *haute cuisine* days, he had many disciples and admirers (including Robert Courtine who for decades was *Le Monde*'s restaurant critic), he was a founder of the journal *Cuisine et Vins de France*, he wrote endlessly about food in famously lucid prose. Some of his best known sayings are as fresh and truthful as ever. *Faites simple*: make it simple. *La cuisine c'est quand les choses ont le gout de ce qu'elles sont*: cooking is when things taste of what they are. You have to remember that this was the heyday of *haute cuisine*, with its endless complicating and mucking about of food.

So, that's Curnonsky. Elected prince in life, forgotten in death. Less than forty years ago. He did call himself a literary mercenary.

In this capacity he wrote more than sixty-five works, which almost to a book haven't stayed in print. And under ten different pseudonyms he published more than a million pamphlets, essays, reports, news items. I used one of his booklets in the very first gastronomic article I ever wrote, for *Epicurean*, about Roquefort.

This seems a roundabout route to take to get to automobile guides, and the forgottenness of Curnonsky is a bit of a detour. I'll explain it by saying that writers have a melancholy interest in the fate of their fellows. All that nocturnal energy of his, sitting scribbling over his prose; all out of print. It's a nightmare. Maybe his day will come again.

BIBENDUM

Back to guides. In Curnonsky, *belle epoque* meets modern technology. In the bar of *Le Journal*, the small daily newspaper he wrote for, he made a *bon mot*: 'There are forty immortals in the Académie française but only one unpuncturable and that's Michelin's.' Meaning of course the tyre. It doesn't sound all that witty now, maybe because it's in English, but when Mr Michelin heard it he was very pleased. The Michelin man, the fat person made of tyres, had just been designed, so Curnonsky was asked to find a name for him. Bibendum, he said, since the Michelin tyre drinks up all obstacles. Cur was at his Latin games again. *Bibendum* meaning drinking up. Like bibulous. Michelin got him to write a weekly bulletin, publicity in disguise, signed Bibendum. This was in 1907.

Cur didn't drive, didn't own a car, had a horror of mechanical things, dreaded speed, but he became counsellor of drivers and celebrator of driving. This was appropriate enough since he was one of the first writers to hail the advent of the car. He saw it born at the end of the century and was full of praise:

By constructing motor cars man has surpassed God for since God exists by nature and by definition outside of all relation to space and time, he is forbidden the joy and the glory of doing 140 an hour. His eternity does not permit him to know the drunkenness of speed and the breaking of records is forever forbidden him.

Curnonsky travelled all over France with various friends, including Marcel Rouff, who wrote *The Life and Passion of Dodin Bouffant*, which might be the world's only gastronomic novel, enjoying the regional cuisine, that simple loving cooking of local specialities that he always preferred to the glitzy overwrought *haute* kind. He was proud of having had a total of twelve accidents, one of which made him *un sinistré du métro*, one of those disaster victims entitled to free métro travel for life.

Curnonsky's cleverness was to make the connection between tourism and gastronomy. When people travelled by train it was to a certain chosen destination; they travelled in order to arrive. But by car you can wander at random, stopping as the fancy takes you. That's when you need advice on the comfort and quality of the accommodations available. And of course you can do the reverse; when there is advice offering, you can choose where to go accordingly. Plan your trip to take you out of your way, to the restaurant worth the journey.

Bibendum the roly-poly Michelin man still beams his pop-eyed smile from the pages of the red and green guides, the red and yellow maps. Michelin tyres still drink up the road. Slightly faster than when Cur described Panhard jumping out of his car after a race of 125 kilometres, waving his top hat and crying in a voice strangled with emotion, We did thirty-eight an hour!

GASTRONOMADES

Curnonsky coined a name for gastronomic tourists. He called them *gastronomades*, making a play of gastronome and nomad, and maybe promenade as well. In the 1950s he celebrated them in another tyre tour guide, this time published by Kleber, for which he wrote a preface, addressing his travellers with grammatical intimacy, as though they are close friends or even soul mates. He describes them scurrying all over France, seeking out little known inns and hostelries where wonderful regional specialities are to be had:

> Pilgrim impassioned of the table, you have traversed foreign countries as well, which has allowed you to make comparisons and to conclude that our France is the paradise of gastronomy …

He goes on to say that gastronomy is a religion in the Latin sense of the word, of a bond between people, and he concludes — Dear younger brothers in feeding — that in this religion they are Grand Priests and certainly the most fervent.

In those days and for several decades more you could say without any fear of dispute — well, somebody might have wondered about China, and just mentioned Italy, but not got away with them — that France was the paradise of gastronomy and nowhere else could come within shouting distance. Were Curnonsky around today … he would continue to believe with most other French people that this is still true.

ROCAMADOUR

Rocamadour isn't exactly on the pilgrim way, but the green guide gives it three stars: it's worth more than a detour, it's worth a special journey. It is a holy place, but it's the combination of the natural drama of the site with human daring that you go to see. It's a cliff face; the plateau stops, in a right angle, and falls straight down to the river 500 metres below. On this vertical surface is built the town of Rocamadour, its churches and chapels, city gates and hotels and fortresses. You could imagine wandering across the difficult terrain of the plateau and tumbling off the edge. Not these days, of course; the lip of the gorge is crowded with hotels and souvenir shops and café terraces with balustrades forming what the French call *belvédères*, lookouts, into the gorge which curves slightly so you can see the limpet-clinging buildings of the old city. This curve in the sides of a deep valley, making a kind of oval circle, is called a *cirque*, a circus; amphitheatre would be a better English word. Such *cirques* are not uncommon in the high plateau country. I always imagine them offering rows of seats for the audiences to the spectacle they themselves create.

Thanks to the red *Michelin* we've chosen a hotel, called la Sainte Marie, the last on the list, so pretty much the cheapest. It has a black bird for quietness, a black arrow for view, a green umbrella with chair and table indicating outdoor eating, plus red brackets round the phrase 'terrace with pleasant view'. None of the others come near this level of excellence, though they are more luxurious and more expensive. One has a red view arrow but it's in l'Hospitalet, the settlement at the top, whose name indicates it was once a hospital, a place of shelter, for pilgrims; an old settlement certainly and the ruins of the hospital still to be seen, but now over-run with the terrible anonymous souvenir shops. That red arrow may indicate that it offers the most famous view, which is of the sunrise shining on the rock, violently lighting it, the guidebook says.

But we prefer to be part of the view, not just look-ing at it, and choosing a hotel in the old city means that we can take the car in, driving in steep sharp zigzags down the cliff, through a tunnel, beside the river, up again along narrow angular streets, through gates of the fortifiable kind. Certain Euro-pean cars are made with retractable wing mirrors so as to negotiate the narrow passages of ancient villages. We crawl through great stone bastions, watching our side mirrors, non-retractable, to see if we are making it. If they can just scrape through, so can we. We're getting in all right, but will we get out? It's comforting to see that there are other cars already here, but their drivers may have long-practised skills that we lack. It seems possible that there will be no place to turn, and we'll have to back out all the way. Tomorrow's problem: think about it then. Unless the hotel is full. It's seven o'clock already.

We park in a narrow street beside the rock face. I have to get out beforehand. If I crane my head back as far as it will go I can see the castle on the top. And birds. Big powerful lazy eagles like hang-gliders catching thermals.

La Sainte Marie can take us. We get a marvellous room. Well, it's basic, and bare, a bed, a chair, some hanging space, a big bathroom, drearily coloured. But one window looks down on to a small square, where steps lead up to the holy city. From the bottom there are 216 steps of this via Sancta, which pilgrims often climbed up on their knees. I'm not sure whether this means literally, like an actor playing Toulouse-Lautrec, or walking up on your feet and kneeling down on each step. Both awkward and painful, and giving you time to reflect on your sins.

Where we are is already 141 steps up — counting the steps seems a thing to do here — and our other window looks steeply down over lower buildings to the river, and across to the other side of the gorge, which has no buildings, only a kind of watch-tower on the road that comes zigzagging across that perpendicular slope. There's a little train that comes down from l'Hospitalet, crosses the river and goes halfway up this other side, stops a while for the view then goes back. In the dark you can see the puny light pricks of camera flashes. Of course it's not really a train, it's a set of little carriages pulled by a small truck, of a kind to become familiar all over the south, as though a train even an imitation one still has some antique glamour. You can hear it labouring as it climbs and stops and climbs a bit more, regularly every hour or whenever. It's the only noise; in between the valley maintains a medieval silence.

Not innocence, though. Outside the several doors of this hotel are almost life-size cut-out people holding menus. There's a pilgrim, in cape, hat, scallop-shells, staff, etcetera; his is sixty-eight francs.

The other figure is a knight, in the usual armour, with his helmet up and a smirk on his face, holding a menu at eighty-eight francs. As well there's the menu of the Val d'Alzou — that's the name of the tiny river whose gentle immemorial wearing away has created this gorge — which is 120 francs, and finally there's *les Fées d'Ouysse* at 210. *Fées* are fairies, and once again I am intrigued by this daily use of the word, which English would find too fey for words. The menu of the Ouysse fairies ... you couldn't say it and remain a serious person. Does this mean that the French have a more childish, or childlike, apprehension? That can accept fairies in the everyday naming of places and things without embarrassment? Or maybe it should remind us of the mysteries of translation, that somehow fairy in English does not have the weight of *fée* in French, though it seems an even more delicate word, and remembering the fearfulness of it as applied to certain powerful women. Like Morgan le Fay, King Arthur's wicked sister, who was always trying to kill him, and dobbed in Lancelot and Guinevere. Or the creatures who appeared at christenings, inflicting gifts of good or evil. Not gauzy little winged things in the gardens of the pixilated, but a figure well grown, beautiful perhaps or unimaginably ugly, an enchantress or a witch.

We don't actually eat any of these menus, not the pilgrim's or the knight's or even the fairies'. Though it's now nine o'clock, lunch-time's roast veal has proved rather rib-sticking. We want a light meal, of elements we have chosen, so we order *à la carte*.

Cosmo has *carpaccio* of salmon. That is, raw, in very thin slices, dressed with a vinaigrette and chives. Followed by a truffle omelette.

TRUFFLES

Here, at Rocamadour, we are in the Périgord, and these are local truffles, the waitress tells us; the market is just down the road. Truffles always make me think of Colette, who said if she couldn't have too many she'd go without. She reckoned they should be eaten like potatoes. With the beginning of the frosty weather she'd have them sent up from the Périgord, clean them herself (she didn't trust anyone else) then cook them in a stewpan with half a bottle of champagne and some fat bacon. You eat the truffles and drink the sauce out of port glasses.

I wonder is there anybody eating this these days? Are there any millionaires taking the trouble? A dish like this for two friends would cost hundreds of dollars. Maybe thousands. Colette makes it sound like a kind of adult dormitory feast, cooked over the sitting-room fire, unexpected, a bit naughty, escaping from the servants who would normally prepare your food.

A truffle omelette is the nearest any of us are ever likely to get to this precious fungus. The thing about truffles is that they give off a powerful scent, and eggs easily take up odours, so the thing to do is put the two together as soon as possible. Break the eggs and slice the truffles in and leave the mixture to rest, or put truffles and whole eggs in a bag together, and you'll have a most wonderfully scented omelette. I have eaten this dish in Australia once, when the chef at Buon Recordo brought in some fresh Italian truffles, the white ones from Piedmont, and made just such an omelette. White truffles are not so highly regarded as black, but this dish was sublime.

CARPACCIO OF SALMON

This is a dish of raw salmon cut in paper-thin slices and served with a vinaigrette. All you need to make it is the ability to cut raw salmon paper thin: using a whole fish and a razor-sharp knife. Some people serve it with capers and a little thin raw onion, but it's spectacular plain.

TOMATO ROSE

Back to Rocamadour. I'm eating a *bloc* of *foie gras*, or some slices from. There is quite a complex hierarchy to *foie gras* which is of largely academic interest outside France: *bloc* is high up, not quite the whole liver freshly cooked in a terrine, not so low as a pâté; it's all liver, but slightly preserved. This one has a thread of truffle in it; I try to taste it but the essential truffle magic is elusive. Maybe if it's really familiar to you this tiny suggestion will evoke it fully again. Or maybe it's given up all its flavour to someone else's omelette. It comes with a perfect tomato rose which is disturbing, considering all the things I've said about the semiotics of radish roses. Followed by a *salade aux noix*, which are walnuts and again very local. The wines come from the region, too, a Bergerac sec, very fine and fruity, and a Cahors, from the Côtes d'Olt. Olt is the old name for the River Lot, before the letters got reversed, being easier to say that way. It remains in some place names. Like St Geniez d'Olt. St Come d'Olt. Lost saints and a garbled river.

NUT SALADS

Make a green salad in the usual way, with whatever variety of leaves pleases, and a vinaigrette dressing made with walnut oil and red wine vinegar. Add walnut halves. This is particularly good made with the leaves of Belgian endive, witloof. For extra richness small cubes of blue cheese can be added.

TERRACE

The evening is balmy, after the hot day, and there's a freshness in this high country air that reminds us of home. After ten, and it's still light. We're sitting on the terrace, looking down over another hotel terrace, lit with large glowing globes on stands like enormous candelabra, farther down to the dark valley, across to the cliff where the pseudo train whines its intermittent journey halfway up, pause, down. And in between the quietness, when you can hear the presence of the earth.

UNCORRUPTED

After dinner we walk up some steps into the holy city, which is not yet locked up, and nearly deserted. More steps and we're in the chapel of Our Lady, the holy of holies. It's hollowed out of the rock, legend says by the hermit who gave his name to this place. Saint Amadour. In the twelfth century one of the locals asked to be buried under the threshold of the chapel, and much later when it was dug up a corpse was found, absolutely intact and uncorrupted. It was put beside the altar for the veneration of the faithful, and there were a number of miracles.

But who was the person in the already ancient sepulchre? An Egyptian hermit? Saint Sylvain? The most popular story, by the the fifteenth century, was that he was the publican Zacharias, the disciple of Christ and husband of Veronica. Veronica being the woman who, as Jesus was climbing to Calvary, wiped his face with her veil, which received in sweat and blood the perfect image of his visage. Vera-Icon: true image. Which makes her, considerably posthumously, the patron saint of photographers. (In fact, I think this derivation of the name is a latter-day invention; it's a mixture of Latin and Greek, for one thing, and what about the inversion of the second syllable?) The actual fabric is a vernicle.

The pass at bullfighting known as the Veronica means the matador's standing immobile and swinging the cape so slowly in the face of the charging bull that it resembles her action of wiping Christ's face.

A veronica may also be a medal imprinted with His face, worn by pilgrims.

Husband and wife, Zacharias and Veronica, settled in the Rocamadour area, and after Veronica's death Zacharias came to the then wild valley of the Alzou.

You have to admire this gallocentrism. France is not very close to Palestine, yet a good many of the players in the first drama of Christianity end up here. As though they know that this is one of the most significant of God's chosen lands. The medieval imagination had all these people travelling the Mediterranean as though there were a ferry most days and a bus to meet it.

Well, legends are good fun. All that is certain about the uncorrupted corpse is that the body under the threshold was a hermit, a familiar of the rock, a lover of the rock, *amator*. And so he was called, in the language of Oc, Amadour. This place is the rock of Amadour.

He had his own pilgrimage. From the first miracles until the Reformation it was one of the most famous in Christendom. There'd be 30 000 people at once, turning the valley of the river into a vast camp. It must have been a bit like Woodstock; not quite so many people but the same problems with the lavatories.

All the best people came: kings, saints. It was a pilgrimage often imposed by ecclesiastical and sometimes civil courts. The penance was severe, and inflicted especially on Albigensians who hated the Mother of God. Pilgrims wore the usual clothes, but on arriving stripped to their shirts and embarked on the knee-climbing of the stairs. With chains hung about necks and arms for extra difficulty.

It was also a place for business trips. The hospices must have offered the medieval equivalent of conference facilities. Nobles and statesmen liked to come to Rocamadour to sign treaties and deeds under the protection of Our Lady. They believed agreements stood a better chance of not being broken if signed in so sacred a place. The town's holy heyday was the thirteenth century; after that it declined, was profaned and devastated. During the Wars of Religion a Protestant captain tried to burn the still uncorrupted body of St Amadour, but it wouldn't catch. Enraged, he took to it with a hammer.

The Black Virgin

The chapel itself was crushed in a rockfall in the fifteenth century, pillaged a number of times with the rest of the city, rebuilt in the nineteenth. It's full of emblems of gratitude, banners, crutches, swords, the pilgrims' penitential irons. Some little boats offered by sailors saved by their prayers to the lady of the chapel swing from the ceiling. And a bell, one of the most ancient known, which rings of its own volition when miracles occur.

But the real miracle is the lady herself, the statue known as the Black Virgin. She is possibly 1100 years old. She is made of walnut wood, originally covered with sheets of silver. The blackness is from centuries of candle smoke. A tall slender maiden, she sits very straight on a wooden seat, and Christ is a small tall child perched on her lap. She holds her head quite high, but looks down on him with a face full of love and wise calm. A face that knows sorrow, the irony of it, and still faintly smiles. You want to look at her, to gaze your fill. So worn she is, so beautiful, so full of her own life. Black she may be, but not sombre; this blackness of a million candles' smoke trembles with their offered-up light. I light a candle myself, a lot of people have before me. She is so moving, this slight medieval girl, so full of power, you could believe in her.

Cosmo takes a photo — illegally, we don't realise till later. It doesn't turn out well, he didn't take account of how small she was, high up there in her grotto, you can hardly see her for gloom. She did not seem like that to the naked eye.

Next morning we visit her again. We can't resist her. We walk about the city on the rock face. Then make our way up to the castle on the edge of the plateau. Not on our knees, nor even by the penitential steps, but taking the lift. A cross between a lift and a cable-car, a vast transparent carriage that slides slowly up a tunnel. You work it yourself, but have to pay.

The castle is nineteenth century, stuck on to a fourteenth-century fort. Its charm is that it is set on the very edge of the cliff so you can walk around its ramparts and look straight down into the valley below. I found this utterly terrifying; I crept on jelly legs, holding tight to the railings. My brain knew this was illogical but my feet didn't; they felt the terrible pull of these eagle-haunted heights. You can go and watch eagles being fed up here, but it's not till four o'clock and we'll be gone by then.

CAHORS

Cahors is one of our favourite French wines, so we have to go and see its name town. Driving across pretty winding mountainous roads. Cahors is a good wine to drink because it doesn't have to be very old; most of the great names need to be cellared before they are at their best, and if they're old enough they cost so much you can't afford them, supposing you could find them. They exist on restaurant menus, but only for the rich, given the expensiveness of age and especially as a mark-up of several hundred per cent isn't uncommon. But Cahors is excellent young. Bottles often have a picture of the old bridge on the label, and here we are, sitting on a kind of dock on the river, eating lunch and looking at it, its forty-metre high towers, its gates, its machicolations. We drove into town and

straight to it, using the red *Michelin* which has
maps, up-to-date ones; our green guide has maps
too but they're about thirty years old, like the prices;
you can laugh when it tells you it'll cost one franc to
visit something and you've just paid twenty-five.

The parking is right on the riverbank, and steps
take you down to the dock — there's a boat offering
river cruises, it's the Lot here — which has tables
and chairs set out. So we succumb and have another
large lunch — fifty francs divided by four makes
$12.50 — of *salade de gésiers*, giblet salad (made of
duck giblets preserved in goose fat, which is a *confit*,
and served hot, with a *confit* of chicken hearts,
served cold, on a straight green salad) and steak
with fried crisp beans and good chips. A plate of
cheese, some sorbet, and wine are included. Plus
coffee which is no good. The beans are snapping
fresh, very green, great handfuls of them stirred in a
pan with oil and garlic, surprisingly good. The steak
thin and full of flavour and juice, tender as well. We
can see all the cooking going on, since the kitchen is
a hole in the wall, rather like a garage, set into the
riverbank under the parking and viewpoint above.
It's called La Guignette de Valentre. It's great luck
finding it, it's the only eating-place in town on the
river. The two youngish men who are working hard
to produce this food are shy, and pleased that we
like it; they tell us how to make the salad, which is,
again, typically local. There are a lot of birds in the
region, ducks, geese, chickens; the favoured cooking
medium is goose fat and after a while it begins
to feel rather disgustingly rich to the foreigner,

especially one who's absorbed warnings about heart disease and animal fat, but the locals live healthily on it and have a low incidence of heart problems. Maybe it's the excellent red wine of Cahors.

THE VALENTRE BRIDGE

You can sit on this dock, and watch the ancient river flow by, and imagine the English galloping up the Lot and failing to take the bridge; the labouring of the cars climbing the steep valley road shows you how hard it would have been for horses to approach; while they picked their way down the hill marksmen on the bridge could pick them off with ease. The French sitting safe on the bridge, watching it happen.

Building of it was begun in 1308; half a century later the architect, filled with despair at its sluggish construction, made a pact with the devil. Satan was to transport all the material necessary and the architect in return would give him his soul. Prodigious results: the bridge is on the point of completion. The architect begins to have second thoughts about eternal damnation. He asks the devil to fetch some water in a sieve. He tries several times, but of course he can't — can't he? I would have thought the devil would have had no problem bringing water in a sieve ... he must have followed the rules for a change. Anyway, he has failed to bring all the materials. So, he admits defeat. But out of revenge he breaks off the pinnacle of the middle tower.

Every time the stone is replaced it falls again. The tower is called the Devil's Tower for this reason.

When the bridge was restored in the nineteenth century the architect made sure the stone was solidly cemented in. On the angle he had carved a small devil trying hard to dislodge it. We can't quite see it from here. And who wants to look too carefully. We want to see the bridge the frustrated English could not capture, not its nineteenth-century restoration.

These devil-tricking stories recur. They're like urban myths, having an underground life of their own, surfacing long distances and many centuries apart. Aachen has one, Aix-la-Chapelle, Charlemagne's marvellous church. The agreement there was for the devil to have the first soul to cross the threshold, in return for quick building. Like all pacts with the devil, it seemed an excellent idea at the time, not so good when the moment of reckoning came. Whose soul would be sacrificed? Nobody was willing to volunteer, nobody wanted to condemn anyone else. Finally they came up with the idea of sending in a pig. The devil was furious, but what could he do? Refused, I'd have thought, said that pigs don't have souls, something like that, but instead he stamped off in a fury, slamming the great bronze doors, and leaving his thumb in one of the doorknob rings — you can feel it to this day. One door has a hollow where the ring goes through the knob, the other has the devil's thumb.

Inside are statues of the pig on one side and its soul on the other — the soul a huge spiked object like a land-mine.

After lunch, into the old town. The cathedral a strange domed church, with paintings, one end quite Gothic. There's a cloister, and a Renaissance court, in the process of being restored. I think being a stonemason and restorer of ancient buildings would be a good trade in France. The Romanesque west door and tympanum are now on the north side and on a busy footpathless street, a medieval street with up-to-the-minute traffic. You risk getting run over as you contemplate. Perhaps joining its haloed Christ sooner than you think.

The town is decorated with banners and there are groups of young energetic people; it seems some pageant, some street theatre is about to occur. We can't wait for it: not for the eagles, or the cruise along the Lot, or the evening's performance. Compostela will not allow such dawdling. We haven't got a lot of time, and the schedule is strict; the car has to be back in Paris, and we have to be back in Australia; these dates aren't flexible.

The people of Cahors are called Caduciens. I find this sympathetic, since coming from Newcastle I am a Novacastrian. Nobody expects the denizens of a scruffy coaly working-class town to be so grand. In Cahors they are Caduciens because the town was called Divona Cardurcorum, which became Cadurca then Cahors. There was a spring here which the Gauls and then the Romans worshipped; it still provides drinking-water for the town. Newcastle people are Novacastrians because some erudite person knew to backform to Latin.

Chasselas

It's hot. In the car. Sixty-two kilometres. To Moissac. One of the highest Romanesque sites. The French have this useful phrase *haut lieu*; high place, in the sense of grand; high spot; a great site that's a great sight. It was originally a hill where the Jews set up sacrificial altars, so it comes to mean a memorable place that has been the scene of high deeds. Here, a great narrative of church building.

The countryside is green and fresh to the eye, there are orchards and vineyards, we have left the grim plateau long behind and are driving through smiling sloping fields. This is the home of table grapes, lovely long clusters of round fruits, of a pearly lustre and slightly golden, deliciously scented and sweet to taste. *Chasselas doré*, gilded Chasselas, known by the name of the town.

Moissac

When you arrive at Moissac on a hot summer afternoon you can sit on a café terrace in the square by the church and order beer and regard the great tympanum which is just there, a metre or so away. You can read it like a book which of course is what it was meant for. The story comes from St John's Vision of the Apocalypse, and this particular narrative is Christ in Glory. His giant figure fills a tall oval in the centre; he's crowned and haloed, his eyes shine, his features are strongly marked, each separate curl of his hair and beard is symmetrically carved, he is a hieratic figure of power and majesty. His right hand is raised in benediction, his left holds the *Book of Life*. You'd better hope your name is written there, when this moment comes.

Round this Christ ruler of the universe are the four apostles, in symbolic form: Matthew the angel, Mark the lion (remember the lions of St Mark's in Venice), Luke the bull, John the eagle. On either side are two tall slender seraphs, reiterating the lovely oval of this central piece. All the remaining space in the tympanum is taken up by old men, twenty-four of them, the kings of the Apocalypse. Each is seated in his own idiosyncratic way, legs crossed, knees splayed, lounging, upright, they hold cups and lutes, each is looking up at the huge stern Christ, the fourteen under his feet having to crane their necks to do so. Their faces show wonder, amazement, fear, and all these gazes fixed with crick-neck difficulty upon the central figure create a powerful dramatic movement in the scene. The central figures may be hieratic, so much so as to become symbols, but the kings of the Apocalypse, or elders some would call them, old men, are full of human agitation. Their job is to begin the melodies that will signal the end of the world.

All this you can see sitting on your café terrace drinking beer and reading the tympanum at Moissac. I'm not normally at all a drinker of beer, but in the summer, when you're hot and thirsty, when you've been driving along in a little car with the windows open and the wind buffeting you about the head, when you want a moment of refreshment so you can go and look at the next lot of beauties, beer seems the perfect drink. French beer, which has a certain elegance of flavour. At this café it's immensely expensive, the owner is no fool, he knows that tourists will pay for his proximity to one of the masterpieces of Romanesque art.

I take Cosmo's photograph, standing in the doorway under the tympanum, beside a carving of an adulterous woman being tortured by demons, toads and serpents. They bite on her breasts and writhe round her genitals. Her mouth is open in an oblong gaping scream that to the Middle Ages must have been as terrible as Munch's. In it is the knowledge of damnation. In the picture Cosmo comes out better than she does, though looking rather worried. But clearly he is flesh and blood and bright colour in the sunlight, while the stone demons have devoured all her substance.

The door jambs here have a curious cusped shape which is quite Islamic, reminding us that we're *en route* to Moorish Spain. The adulterous woman's elongated writhing echoes the diagonal lines of the cusps.

The other marvel to see in Moissac is the cloister. A large arcaded space of palpable peace, full of simple light and clarity. The stone arches, the plain triangles of grass, the immense cedar, the hazy light: it's a place to be, not to do. Even occasional trains racketing past can't touch its dense and luminous calm. Though they nearly did for it altogether; in the nineteenth century it was planned to knock the whole thing down to allow passage for the railway line from Bordeaux to Sète.

Of course you have to remember that the French Revolution coming on top of the Wars of Religion and the Hundred Years War had left the buildings in a sorry mess. The revolution condemned the Church along with the aristocrats; first it was secularised and then suppressed, its treasures pillaged, its archives dispersed. Moissac was left derelict. Demolishing what was left to put through a railway might not have seemed like vandalism. The age of steam after all had its own cathedrals, in the form of magnificent railway stations, and we've already had occasion to mourn the demolition of many of these.

Now, at Moissac, you enter the cloister through a fine new building, with space for exhibitions and a shop selling books and moderately tasteful souvenirs and anything at all appropriate. And a till. We are all prepared to pay to taste the ancient peace of the cloister. Not all of us are going to Compostela, but we are all pilgrims seeking the absolution of the past. We've travelled to get it. Listen to the languages: English, German, something Scandinavian, the particular kind of French that Canadians speak. And not only foreigners, there are plenty of France's own people seeking out their past. As we are doing. Christendom took no note of national boundaries, and it is as members of Christendom that we are here. Its works of art are our heritage. Belief in the religion that fostered them is not essential; faith in the common humanity of those who made them and of us who want to look at what they made is what counts.

St Bernard's criticism of cloisters

The arches of cloisters are held up by columns, and these columns have capitals, which often have marvellous carvings, not always religious, sometimes simply decorative, at other times fabulous, with strange beasts and mysterious creatures. They may tell comical stories, or small narratives of daily life, or the terrible myths of the Bible, the sacrifice of Isaac, Noah's drunkenness, Eve offering the apple. The shafts of the columns may have complicated entwining patterns, for the finger to trace and the eye to lose itself in. There may be panels with portraits, of bishops or saints. St Bernard, an austere man, complained about this decoration, in 1127:

> But in the cloister, under the eyes of the brethren who read there, what profit is there in those ridiculous monsters, in that marvellous and deformed comeliness, that comely deformity? To what purpose are those unclean apes, those fierce lions, those monstrous centaurs, those half-men, those striped tigers, those fighting knights, those hunters winding their horns? Many bodies are there seen under one head, or again, many heads to a single body. Here is a four-footed beast with a serpent's tail; there, a fish with a beast's head. Here again the forepart of a horse trails half a goat behind it, or a horned beast bears the hinder quarters of a horse. In short, so many and so marvellous are the varieties of divers shapes on every hand, that we are more tempted to read in the

> marble than in our books, and to spend the whole
> day in wondering at these things rather than in
> meditating the law of God. For God's sake, if men
> are not ashamed of these follies, why at least do
> they not shrink from the expense?

St Bernard might have deplored the monks' gazing
at cloisters rather than reading in their pious books,
but how lovingly his words evoke their beauty.
They belie his intentions. But you can see why his
writing was called 'a river of Paradise'. Bernard was
very holy. People knew straight away that he was a
saint; they canonised him in 1174, only twenty years
after his death, and in 1830 he was declared a doctor
of the Church: *Doctor mellifluus*, the honey-sweet
Doctor, is how he is named.

CHAMPAGNE

St Bernard's home abbey, at Clairvaux, was in
Champagne; his monks cultivated vines and made
their own wine. They got a measure of wine for
every meal, because it was thought to keep them in
good health. And perhaps on St Benedict's grounds,
that it is 'better to take a little wine of necessity than
a great deal of water with greed'. The monks of
south-western France took generations to restore the
vineyards which the Moors had destroyed in the
eighth century; they drained the swamps of the
Médoc and planted vines there. Much of the mag-
nificence of the Cluniac monastery at Moissac was

owing to its trade in wine. Wine and God frequently went together.

In St Bernard's time the wine of Champagne was a still wine, and remained so for some centuries. It became very popular with the kings of France, and had a reputation for making people cheerful.

The champagne with bubbles that we know owes something to the pilgrimage to Compostela. Not everything, but something. The best wine was made at the Abbey of Hautvillers, which owned an important relic, the body of St Helena, mother of the Emperor Constantine. As was a common practice, she'd been stolen from Rome by a priest of Rheims, in 841, and as also was usual, seemed happy in her new home. She did all sorts of miracles, including sending rain when the wine-growers prayed for it. Pilgrims came to see the relics, bringing gifts, the abbey grew rich, acquired more vineyards. The moment was ripe for Dom Perignon, a scholarly scientific monk whose eyesight had failed from much study but who had a superb palate and could tell from tasting grapes which vineyard they came from, and which other wines they could be mixed with, and was never wrong.

He had the idea of using the secondary spring fermentation that made this wine effervescent, to control it, the moment of it, and to keep it in the wine. The way to do this was in the bottle, and this is where Compostela comes in. He could manage this fermentation in the bottle because he used cork stoppers. Corks had been around in Roman times, but people had forgotten about them. One of the monks from Hautvillers went to Compostela (perhaps checking out a rival pilgrimage?), brought back some corks from Spain, and Dom Perignon was able to make champagne as we know it.

That's why Moet and Chandon, who in 1794 bought the remains of the Abbey of Hautvillers which had been destroyed during the revolution, and the vineyards which hadn't, give Dom Perignon's name to their best wine. To honour guests, they will open a bottle of a significant year, a birthday, an anniversary. When I went in 1991 it was a 1978 vintage, because I was Australian, and 1978 was sort of connected to the founding of the country. You don't worry too much about logic when somebody's pouring you a glass of 1978 Dom Perignon. The approximation is because the wine isn't made every year, only when the grapes are good enough. Even the Queen Mother on her visit had to make do with the vintage before her birth year — of course, it was pretty old.

WINE AND GOD

This lovely phrase isn't mine, it belongs to Maguelonne Toussaint-Samat, who has written a marvellous history of food. She explains how it was monks and monasteries who were responsible for the wine we drink today; they grew a bit for religious purposes (wine being found wherever Mass is sung), a bit more for hospitality purposes, a bit more for the health of their own people, and then for trade, export, revenue. They were doing it for the glory of God, so they wanted it to be as perfect as possible.

And not just monks in monasteries, nuns in nunneries; sometimes doing the work themselves, sometimes hiring people. They were good at it, not only making excellent wines but distributing them cleverly. The business of wine was sometimes at threat from barbarians, but one good thing came out of their pillaging: people hid their barrels of wine in the cellar, thus making the revolutionary discovery, wine likes being in a cellar. Says Toussaint-Samat, 'Being stored in attics had done it no good at all.'

Other latter-day barbarians wiped out wine-growing altogether: Calvin in Switzerland and Henry VIII in England. Their Protestant reforms put a stop to viticulture. That's the most damning indictment of Protestantism I've ever heard.

There are more than thirty saints connected with wine, especially martyrs, their spilled blood having a special affinity with the blood of the grape. And of course being a humbler version of the Mass, the blood of Christ. St Vincent (vin = wine — sounds like sympathetic nomenclature), St Martin, St Bacchus ... he seems unlikely, but is supposed to be real, a German called Bach. He was the patron saint of the vines on the Mont Valérien, at Suresnes, on the edge of Paris, and used to be beaten every year at the vintage. Ritual beating of saints, of course in effigy, who hadn't sent the right weather was common; St Bacchus' punishment seems to have been in case he didn't behave well.

In Burgundy the great Clos-Vougeot was originally a priory. Petrarch reckons that Pope Urban V was not at all keen to leave it and return to Rome for fear of being deprived of this even then magnificent wine. The local motto is, He who drinks good wine sees God.

RENOIR

A footnote, this. Renoir liked to paint people enjoying themselves at jolly establishments on the banks of the Seine, called *guingettes*. I've seen various meanings given to this word, that they are boat restaurants, waterside cafés, and such. Toussaint-Samat remarks that ordinary people usually drank second-pressing wine, thin stuff called *piquette*. Also known as *guignet*, acid, and since it was drunk in public houses along the Seine these got called *guingettes*.

And so our hole-in-the-wall restaurant in Cahors. Though the wine was a little better than *guignet*.

The drinker of good wine sees God. Whoever drinks a pint of the wine of Montmartre, says a proverb, will piss four.

BENIGHTED

We're planning to spend the night at Moissac. I've got a decent-sounding place picked out of the red guide, nothing glamorous, so reasonably priced. No birds or brackets or little green seats, but there aren't any round here. It's about seven o'clock; we leave the car parked by the church and walk across the market square.

On the way we pass a Timy, a brand of supermarket we're familiar with from other trips to the south; we'll buy some fruit and cheese and wine, and there's a bakery next door, to make a picnic in the hotel room. I like picnics in hotel rooms. We've got some wine glasses I bought at Printemps in Paris, and a corkscrew; we can go to bed early. Maybe there'll be something on television.

Disaster. The hotel is full. Very sorry. Coach parties. *Cars* is the french word. *Beaucoup de cars*. The woman at the desk is kind. She rings up several others. All full. A lot of coach parties. It is the middle of June. Try Valence, along the road to Agen. We haven't actually planned the next stage. Agen? It's northish as well as west ... Okay. On to Valence. We rush off, no time to see any more of Moissac, only a glimpse of the massive Tarn, broad-flowing river we've known in its beginnings, way over in the Gorges, and the calm canal. Canals are wonderfully calm, it's their straight-ruled banks. Or perhaps the serenity comes from their easy life, having everything done for them, not having to carve their own way over millennia, like rivers.

Pity about Timy. No time to buy picnics.

What about somewhere along the road? The small places not in the guide, the friendly looking restaurants with rooms: taverns, inns, whatever. Suddenly there don't seem to be any. Valence, then.

It stands in the lee of huge gas tanks, Cosmo remembers thirty years ago and the French government's educational trips for foreign students: Moissac's cloister and tympanum but also natural gas installations. They smell unpleasant.

Valence isn't big but it's complicated. Not big enough for a map in the *Michelin*, but big enough to get lost in. The driver gets cross with the navigator. The navigator shouts at the driver for missing last-minute turns. The tour manager ought to have thought of getting the hotel on first arriving in Moissac, the church would have kept. Why didn't the driver think of it, then? The atmosphere in the car is tense. It's hard arriving in a town of some 80 000 people and trying to find a hotel. After considerable bad temper we manage to. It's called the Tout Va Bien, which means Everything's Going Well. And so it is, for the Tout Va Bien. It's full. So is everywhere else in the town. It's the summer.

We're beginning to feel seriously benighted. What if there simply isn't anywhere? We can't sleep in this skimpy little car. Agen, then, as fast as possible. All we know about Agen is that it's where the prunes come from.

Well, we end up at something called a Stim'Otel, modern, dull, clean, a lift. Very badly designed. So exiguous, and you can't forgive it because it's a new building and designed like that. Open the window abruptly and you break the lamp which is low down on the wall beside the bed. As usual there are no shower curtains or screens so the bathroom floods. It can't be good for the fabric of the building. Not that we wish the fabric of this building any good.

Pokiness is okay in an ancient edifice: such atmosphere, you can't expect convenience as well. They've done the best they could in difficult circumstances. But in a new building you get furious that they didn't bother to get their measurements right. At least it's in *centre ville*: the middle of town. The dining-room looks like a failed English teashop. Most likely dinner's off, anyway, at this hour, closer to ten than nine. The remaining diners look depressed. We go for a walk and find a place to eat.

LA BOHEME

It's a small restaurant, a narrow room, some tables on the pavement in a small street, an alley really. They bring us a lovely cold dry white wine, quite local. The menu makes us think of an Australian restaurant. It's only a list of names, but it captures the imagination. French menus are familiar, like rhymes learned in childhood. There may be variations, but the only surprise is an unexpected old refrain. At least that's how we feel after our days' driving south. Whereas this menu reads like a book we've not seen before, though the words of course are familiar. It's ideal for people tired and grumpy and still getting over the fright of benightment, although we also wish we had huge appetites and could eat a lot.

I choose a salad of various greens, with small spicy black puddings, garnished with sautéed apple, a version of the sort of *salade tiède* which *nouvelle cuisine* made fashionable and which is one of my favourite dishes. As is black pudding. Cosmo has a brilliant fish dish.

PERSILLADE DE POISSON

Madame of the restaurant gave me this recipe but not precisely; really only a description. She made it with layers of fish: cod, salmon, trout she mentioned, and lots of herbs.

I used 300 g ocean perch, 300 g salmon, 300 g red fish. Another time I used some sort of dory instead of the ocean perch. Any three pleasant-tasting fish will do; the salmon is good for the colour.

Cut the fish fillets crosswise in thin slices. Put a layer of ocean perch in an oblong loaf tin, then a layer of salmon, a layer of red fish. Sprinkle with a good quantity of finely chopped herbs — I used chives, dill, parsley and sorrel. Pour over lemon juice (I used 1½ juicy lemons). Keep going in the same pattern until all the fish is used up, finishing with herbs and lemon. Cover with cling film, and weight (use a tin of beans or something like that — I've got a little plastic drawer full of nails that I put in a plastic bag, it's a good shape). Leave overnight.

Cut into slices, not too thin, and serve. It actuall cuts remarkably well. An immensely impressive dish. And of course the fish isn't raw, the lemon juice actually cooks it.

Serves 8.

Salade Tiede

Being an invention of *nouvelle cuisine*, warm salads are rather old-fashioned now, which is a good reason for eating them.

Basically you make a salad of greens with a well-flavoured vinaigrette dressing and pour some sizzling hot meat or fish over it. Caesar salad is one version, with its cos lettuce, croûtons, parmesan cheese, egg, and bacon fried. A favourite of mine is curly endive, especially the very young variety available now, served with garlic croûtons, or small rounds of French bread toasted and rubbed with garlic (which makes them very powerfully flavoured), and small pieces of bacon or pancetta fried (you can add cubes of Gruyère cheese to this and you have a meal). Just as it is cooked you deglaze the pan with some balsamic vinegar — or wine or sherry vinegar — plus a little white wine, or sherry, or vermouth, and pour over the salad so that it wilts just a little. Spinach is good with a similar combination, and also with ham diced, and a very mustardy dressing. A mixture of green leaves, especially with some slightly bitter ones, is good with pieces of hot diced chicken and some onion melted with it, deglazed and poured over; maybe with some mushrooms as well, or avocado tossed with the greens. Duck breasts are a possibility. Prawns, or scallops: *coquilles St-Jacques* make a lovely dish. And of course if you could find some tiny black puddings you could make the one I ate at La Bohème, the little *boudins* cooked with pieces of apple that were glazed with the pan juices.

The only expertise you need to make a good warm salad is a little thought, to combine a variety of greens with a vinaigrette, herbs, hot titbits, and such, so as to arrive at interesting flavours. You can often make a good cupboard or refrigerator salad of this kind: you open the door and see what you've got. In a strict way, not shoving everything in, paying attention to what goes with what.

AUSTRALIAN

It's still warm, sitting in the narrow old street looking at the house with *colombages* over the way, *colombages* being half-timbering, dark wood with rose-pink bricks. There's a dull shop underneath. People pass by, and occasionally a car tries to drive down, but thinks better of it. Several tables away is a group of English people, a man with a wife who says nothing and drinks coke (How do you know she's his wife, asks Cosmo; I can tell by the way she sits beside him. He passes her things in a bossy possessive dismissive fashion), another man who talks so pompously and portentously, so loudly that even people who don't understand his English can tell that he's a bombastic idiot. It makes you want to carry a sign saying *Australien*. We make sure we tell the woman serving where we come from. Her husband is the cook, this is their venture, though there is an old family establishment in the Périgord. La Bohème: it's a curiously old-fashioned romantic name for a place rethinking and reinterpreting the die-hard classics.

NOT COMPOSTELA?

It was at Rocamadour that I said to Cosmo, What if we don't go to Compostela? I'm the navigator, he drives. I've taken a careful calculating look at the map, seen how far we've come, how far we have to go. All the marvellous Romanesque stopping places. The heat. The small car. You could make it if you got on a motorway and put your foot down, but then you wouldn't see anything. Isn't that the object of the journey? And the car doesn't like motorways, too many too fast trucks, too dirty, fumy, noisy, and you have to have the windows down. It likes small roads, winding, leafy, the empty countryside where hidden people live. Where side roads and signposts point to ancient habitation. We're with the car on this.

It's too terrible a thought to contemplate. Not go to Compostela? We have planned it. This and the string of pilgrim stages across the north of Spain are the fixed and certain points of the itinerary. We can wander back and forth through France, as pilgrims did, choosing one of the four routes, or mixing them up, but once across the Pyrénées, at Puente la Reina, there is only one way, from village to hamlet to town, town to hamlet to village, each with its church or abbey or tower or hospice, to the far Atlantic coast, and Compostela where the scallops grow.

PENITENCE

Pilgrimages were at first a penance for sins. The greater the sin the more distant and perilous the journey. Or if you couldn't make it difficult by distance, because the infidel had invaded the Holy Land, or you didn't have the time, you could add handicaps, like going up the 216 steps of Rocamadour on your knees. Brigands did their bit to add to the danger. And the cold and violent storms of the Auvergne often carried people off. So did the difficult snows and mountain passes of the Pyrénées. Though death on a pilgrimage must have been more holy than most. You could surely count on grace if you died in such an enterprise.

But pilgrimages could be devotional as well as penitential, designed to store you up riches in heaven. Building a credit balance of goodness, rather than countering a debit of sins. And the devotional could become festive, as in Chaucer's pilgrimage, where as sinful a bunch of people as you could hope to meet set off to go to Canterbury, with songs and feasting and lots of good yarns, since the whole trip is a pretext for Chaucer's collected stories.

Almost the first class I went to at university was on Chaucer, and I still remember how thrilling was the lecturer's reading of its first lines. He was a good actor, and read them well; he seduced me.

Whan that Aprille with his shoures soote
The droghte of March hath perced to the roote,
And bathed every veyne in swich licour

Of which vertue engendred is the flour
Whan Zephirus eek with his sweete breeth
Inspired hath in every holt and heeth
The tendre croppes, and the yonge sonne
Hath in the Ram his halve cours yronne
And small fowles maken melodye
That slepen al the nyght with open ye
(So priketh hem nature in hir corages)
Then longen folk to go on pilgrimages

The singing of the small birds that sleep all night with their eyes open, because nature has caused their hearts to ache, the sweet showers of April piercing to the root of March's drought, the liquorous sap rising in the veins of plants and bringing flowers to birth, the sweet breath of the wind god breathing life into crops, all this under the sign of the ram, Aries...

It's very sexy poetry this; plants, animals, are full of life and quickening, they're fecund and fertile, the sap rises, the blood sings, the heart aches, in a pleasurable way of course, because it is full of desire and desire is what we all yearn for. So the pilgrims set off on a spring holiday. With bawdy jokes and romantic stories and erotic ones and vulgar and adventurous.

'...then longen folks to go on pilgrimages.' Perhaps the reading of those gorgeous words to a prim sixteen-year-old needing something for her heart to ache over, perhaps that was the beginning of my fascination with the narrative journeyings of the pilgrimage.

PICNIC

At last, we get to a town before the shops shut and manage to buy some lunch. A *baguette de campagne*, delicious densely flavoured bread that you can buy all over France now, some ethnic pâté, heavy and porky, a small pot of *salade niçoise* which is far from home and shows it (Sydney is closer to Nice when it comes to making a good *salade niçoise* than most of France) and a punnet of raspberries. We stop by the side of a river, on a kind of low wide gravelled space, with small trees. The river, it seems to be the Baise, rising in the Pyrenees and flowing north to the Garonne, here is wide and slow moving. Ahead is a bridge and beside a weir a large flour mill, very nineteenth century, but dusty whitened tankers come and go. We walk along the bank and pick mirabelles off the ground, where they've fallen from a tree above a high wall. Sweet and tart together, hot and bursting from the sun.

The name of this town is Condom. I have to confess I couldn't resist posting a pile of cards for the sake of the postmark.

SALADE NICOISE

Purists are very strict about what does and does not constitute a true *salade niçoise* but since they all disagree I would take no notice. Though there are certain necessary elements. Tuna, tomatoes, for instance. Here's a basic one.

Make a vinaigrette of olive oil and a dash of vinegar (I mix these much as purists do martinis: one part in five is pretty vinegary for me), mix in a big wide bowl. Thinly slice a sweet onion and a clove of garlic, toss in vinaigrette. Add handfuls of green leaves — cos, mignonette — toss. Slice cucumbers, tomatoes, quarter hard-boiled eggs, spread over lettuce leaves. Sprinkle with olives. Basil if you have it. Open a tin or two of excellent tuna, in olive oil preferably, turn out in middle of salad.

You can add some thin crisp green beans if you wish. Some people like potato: simply tuna, potato, olives, onions is very good. And try poaching your own fresh tuna, but don't overcook it, or it will be dry.

Restaurants char-grill tuna sometimes and serve it on a salad, but this is being fancy. A good dish for a barbecue though.

On a summer night, when you can't think what to have for dinner, a big bowl of *salade niçoise* is excellent. It tastes good, very fresh, it's filling, and virtuous.

FRUIT IS DESTINY

The warm mirabelle bursting on the tongue. It is summer, and hot, hot. Australia, and summer in December, six months and the other side of the world away from pilgrimages in France. And it's Christmas as well. I think having summer every year is a bit too often, so every six months is excessive. When I came to live in Canberra people said, You'll be cold there, and cold is still the word most frequently used for it, when climate is mentioned, yet in these days of the summer solstice the temperature has been quivering around forty degrees Celsius, a dry searing droughty high-country heat that has defeated even its famously cool nights.

And the winters … they're heated. In buildings and cars the temperature is controlled. It may be frosty in the mornings (minus nine this year, which did for the lemons; they can't cope past minus eight, they go spongy and juiceless) but mostly during the day the sun shines; you sit in a warm room looking out at a sunlit landscape and winter doesn't seem so bad. Well, if you're not a road-mender or a window-cleaner.

The last time I was seriously cold was in Poitiers, another December, three years ago. We'd come from La Rochelle in a slow train, hours in a heatless empty carriage. First class, because we had Eurail passes, and once you're over twenty-five you're obliged to buy first class. Getting off the train we discovered that economy class was warm and full of passengers.

So we arrived bone-cold, in this small town with its various medieval beauties all within walking distance of one another, and set out to see them. We stood outside the magnificent west front of Notre Dame de la Grande, with its three thirteenth-century portals and as many tympanums, tympani, one of them to St Thomas, who's the patron saint of stonemasons, and miraculous builder of a mystic palace for the king of India. A façade that needs a lot of reading, so many pictures does it offer, and we jumped up and down to try to keep our blood moving. The guidebook describes this façade as a vast sculpted page, and gives it three stars; it demanded more than a quick glance. Poitiers has a number of churches, and inside them was a fine ancient cold stored in stone over centuries, outside was a sharp new-minted iciness, whether continental or Atlantic, from east or west, I'm not sure. Walking however briskly from church to church didn't help. We expected to be able to slip into cafés and warm ourselves inside and out — all we'd had was a cold sandwich brunch on the train — but there didn't seem to be any. A curiously café-less city, Poitiers; maybe it's the long finger of English influence down the centuries. Belonging with the Plantagenet style of the architecture. Anyway, I have a fondness for it, as providing my only memory of being truly cold in the last decade or so.

Back to heat. Canberra in December. Warm fruit in the sun. Our friends Judy and Neil have gone to the coast. Once everyone in Canberra went to the coast in December, now only a lot of people do. Neil said we might like to pick their cherries; the Kentish cherry tree, which some tenants considering the fruit inedible had tried to cut down but fortunately not succeeded, Neil having with some trouble saved it, the Kentish cherry was loaded with fruit which would be exactly ripe in a week. The fruit is small, with tiny seeds, it's a light clear scarlet colour and very pretty, it gladdens the heart to see this gnarled and tumbledown tree all covered in tiny red globes.

Neil had told Nancy about the fruit too. Nancy's the person in *Eat My Words* who grew up in Goulburn, in a family of ten children, and whose summers were dogged by the chore of fruit bottling. We were students together in Bruce Hall, more than thirty years ago. The other day, her own children grown and gone, she sold her Fowlers Vacola fruit-bottling equipment. It was a symbolic as well as a practical gesture. I have given up preserving fruit, she said. I have done enough of it in my lifetime. I have paid my dues to fruit.

On 27 December she rang me up. We should go and pick those cherries, she said. They're too beautiful to leave to rot.

I'd been keen in theory, but the act ... it's a nuisance ... I'm writing a book...

Well, we go. At five o'clock, with a handful of plastic bags. The cherries are easy to pick because the tree is low, thanks to the vandals who nearly destroyed it utterly. We have a lovely time. Maybe the season helps, this space between Christmas and New Year, a kind of off-the-calendar time when little work is done, unless you are a shop assistant in the post-Christmas sales. Or a person writing a book. The cherries slip off the stalks with ease (later we discover that most of the recipes tell us to leave the stalks on), the sun is not too hot, and we can talk in a pleasant idle way. We never have time to talk properly: hurried on the telephone because we're both at work (Nancy is more conscientious at brevity than

me because I'm self-employed), in terse asides at
meetings where there is serious business to discuss;
even if we drive to them in the same car in order to
have time to talk it's talk about the meetings, like as
not. Here in this late-sunny orderly garden, with its
vegetables in rows, its murmur of chooks, its tomatoes tall and staked, unripe because however hot this
is the high country and tomatoes never ripen before
the New Year, its artichokes in thistle bud and its
vast tree of plums thankfully not ripe, we don't want
those on our conscience too, we can pick fruit and
murmur our way through the meandering paths of
old conversations. When we were young we were
housewives, we brought up our children and played
with them, we cooked good meals for our families
and elaborate ones for our guests, we sewed things
on sewing machines and behaved much as our
mothers had done. And we lived in different cities so
we did none of these things together. Now we have
jobs that don't fit into tidy working hours, and that
old busy leisure, full of the doing of useful things
that we had chosen, is no more. Nancy's daughter
has three children under the age of seven, works
four days a week, and is doing an MA in her spare
time. Nancy and I look at one another. And we
thought we were busy, we say. Yet we were, in a
fruitful, thrifty, short-of-money, self-organised way.
Now, picking cherries, industrious, provident,
happy (wallowing in race memory, you might say),
we live for a moment in the lives of women who
have enjoyed such work in company and conversation. Work must often have been like this. A kind of

idyll. I think it often was for Aboriginal women, who gathered food and prepared it, and told stories, and laughed. In an unhurried way, knowing there was time to do it, for the tasks to be performed at their own right speed, and enjoyed. This might sound as if I'm idealising, romanticising; I don't think so. It was industrialisation that turned work into a chore, that sweated women's labour in meaningless fragmented tasks. Aboriginal women knew nothing of that. Our mothers were often isolated, so that they didn't have the fun of company, but sometimes they managed it. Nancy remembers her mother talking about going on cherry-picking expeditions, in a group, and afterwards sitting stoning the cherries one by one with a hairpin, and laughing and having a great time that she recalled seventy years later. Aboriginal women did that all the time.

The fecund vegetable plots are separated from the rest of the garden by a trellis. On it Neil is growing blackberries (a special domestic kind, no pests these) which are still green, and raspberries, which are ripe. Some indeed have ripened and then desiccated, they hang shrivelled on their canes. We worry; Neil hasn't mentioned raspberries, but duty tells us not to leave them self-destructing. Maybe somebody else is picking them, says Nancy. They're not doing much of a job then, I say. We pick the ripe raspberries. And spy, under their leaves, clusters of redcurrants. More worry. But we pick them too. Redcurrants are too rare a treat to leave to rot.

Of course, picking is only the half of it. There's the preserving. I find a marvellous nineteenth-

century recipe for pickling redcurrants in themselves. Next morning I'm pottering round the
kitchen with sugar and vinegar and stainless steel
saucepans and two tiny pots for my clusters of redcurrants. I'm just discovering that I've put too much
salt in (how could I have forgotten that I'm out of
the habit of salt?) when Nancy comes.

She's been picking apricots. One of her sons is
living in a house with an enormous tree covered
with apricots. He's too busy to do anything with
them ... You can't leave apricots to rot, can you?

She's picked bags and bags full. She's brought
one for me. Kilos of fruit. She's not sure how she's
going to cook them yet. I show her the beautiful red-
currant recipe: it's in *The Penguin Book of Jams, Pickles
and Chutneys* by David and Rose Mabey.

I used to have one of those, she says. I gave it
away. Because I wasn't going to need it any more.

Ah, I say. Fruit is destiny. Your destiny, anyway.

She copies out the recipe for pickled redcurrants.
This is it.

PICKLED REDCURRANTS

You need a mixture of bunches and single
fruit. [The quantities aren't given — it's really a
couple of handfuls.] Boil the single berries in a mixture of 100 g sugar, 1 cup white wine, 1/2 cup wine
vinegar and 1 heaped teaspoon salt until a good
colour is obtained. Skim it well and let it get cold.
Strain and push as much of the fruit through the sieve

as possible. Boil again and skim until clear. Put the bunches in glass jars and pour the hot liquid over to cover. Seal with paper.

Good with ham, or cold lamb.

Part of its charm is its beauty.

I said that this recipe came originally from the Mabeys' book. They got it from *The Art and Mystery of Curing, Potting and Preserving* by A Wholesale Curer of Comestibles, Chapman & Hall, 1864.

Here is Nancy's recipe for:

SUMMER PUDDING

Summer pudding is a combination of good plain ingredients — white bread and the new season's fruit. If made (as is traditional) with a combination of raspberries and redcurrants it is decidedly luxurious and makes an excellent alternative to Christmas pudding — but other fruits may be used alone or in combination (blueberries, other berries, stoned plums — but not strawberries which seem to acquire a musty taste very quickly).

Remember that colour is part of the appeal. Some fruit needs cooking, other just steeping.

For a good shape, make your pudding in an old-fashioned pudding basin (up to 1.5 litre capacity). Choose your basin according to the volume of fruit available — you need enough fruit to fill the basin rather more than three-quarters full.

Use raspberries, redcurrants (no more than one-quarter the weight of the raspberries), enough caster sugar to sweeten the fruit; perhaps half a loaf of day-old white bread (a square sandwich loaf is best — you could even used sliced bread). [Don't do what I did and use classy Italian — too solid and holey at once. And never use a fancy bread like brioche.]

For safety place a square of waxed paper in the bottom of the basin, so the points come a little way up the sides. Bring the redcurrants to the boil, take off heat, sweeten them generously and pour them while very hot over the raspberries. Stir and check for sweetness — add extra caster sugar if necessary. Allow to cool a little — there will be quite a lot of juice. Slice the bread evenly, cut off the crusts and line the bottom and walls of the basin carefully with the bread — no gaps, no overlap. Spoon the fruit into the 'crust' but reserve most of the juice. Make a bread lid and tuck it round so there are no gaps. Spoon a little of the juice on top to moisten it. Weight the pudding (a saucer with a jar of jam on top?).

Refrigerate for at least 24 hours. Before serving loosen the sides gently, and turn out. Peel off the paper. If the surface is not uniformly pink, use a little of the reserved juice to moisten the white patches. Serve with any remaining juice and thin unsweetened cream.

Dead easy.

And the big bag of apricots? I thought I'd done apricots in *Eat My Words*. Especially a good *tagine*, a savoury meat dish. And why not just cut them in halves and stew them for a few minutes, with a dash of sugar? Nancy served these, when she had us for dinner; this was a having-families-for-dinner occasion, not a dinner party (we'd begun with a barbecue, of lamb kebabs with yoghurt, mint and garlic). She put out a bowl of stewed apricots, some raspberries and cherries quickly cooked together (the cooking of fruit should be really speedy, otherwise you'll have mush without much flavour) with some custard left over from the Christmas pudding, some whipped cream, and a plate of the little macaroons called *Amaretti di Saronno*. And she just happened to have a bottle of Amaretto liqueur (for so long she couldn't remember where it came from) for dipping the biscuits in. It was a feast. People would eat a little of this, and that, try combinations. Stewed fruit is a homely pleasure that should not be forgotten.

For more grandeur, here's a kind of *tarte Tatin*, which is the famously difficult apple pie made by the Tatin sisters, in their equally famous restaurant. Their originality was to put the apples underneath the pastry, and caramelise them. This dish uses apricots. You could call it *tarte Tatin aux abricots*, or

UPSIDE-DOWN APRICOT TART

 You need a flame-proof china or glass or metal pie plate to make this in.

PASTRY
200 g flour

100 g butter
1 teaspoon sugar
cold water

FILLING
750 g apricots
75 g butter
200 g sugar

Make the pastry with the flour, butter and sugar, mixing to the desired texture with cold water. Leave in a cool place. Cut the apricots in half and remove the stones. Put 50 g butter in the pie dish, put over heat until just melted. Sprinkle with a thick layer of sugar (about 100 g). Arrange the apricot halves in the dish, round part in the sugar. Cook for about 15–30 minutes (you may want to use a heat diffuser) until the sugar caramelises and the apricot juice evaporates. Sprinkle on the remainder of sugar and butter in pieces.

Roll out the pastry and spread over the top, tucking in the edges.

Cook at 230°C in a preheated oven for 30–35 minutes. Take the tart out of the oven and after about 10 minutes turn it out on to a serving plate. It will unmould easily. Serve it warm.

The tricky part is the caramel, to get the sugar brown but not too burnt by the time the pie is cooked. The main thing is to keep an eye on it — difficult, since it's upside down, but it seems to work very nicely. You can use less butter and sugar, it won't be so rich.

As for the cherries, you'd have to say that they weren't very exciting. They tasted quite pleasant, and helped to fill my summer pudding. They were okay as stewed fruit for breakfast on cereal. But their taste couldn't match their beauty on the tree. Nancy reckons they're Persian, that they are those tiny red fruits that hang from branches in walled Paradise gardens, painted with luminous precision like the jewels of the women and the patterns in the carpet. That's what we should do with the Kentish cherries, she says: admire them on the tree like a Persian painting.

REDNESS

If redness has a smell it's the smell of raspberries. Not strawberries or apples or radishes or chillies, though they are all very red in their way. There is the redness of wine, but this is an artefact, even perhaps a creation of high art. The elaboration and subtlety of the process removes it from pure redness into shades of purple and brown, its taste no longer has the simplicity of pure red. No, the real essence of redness is in raspberries, uncompromising yet ambiguous, able to absorb sugar to form shining ruby jellies, so you are reminded of the excellent old magic of this demonised industrial white crystal, yet retain its own strong tartness. Its pungency. You can make synthetic raspberry but one whiff will tell you how desperately short of the real thing it falls. Last night I saw a programme on the television about making robots to do everything that humans can do, to feel and have emotions (especially to look after Japan's increasing numbers of old people) but this morning, smelling the redness of raspberries and cherries cooked for three minutes with a sprinkle of sugar, I don't believe it. If you can't synthesise the smell of raspberry redness, how can you mechanise a human conscience?

SUMMER FEAST

Before I leave the antipodean summer: what savoury foods to eat at Christmas? In my teaching days I gave a class an essay to write on Christmas in winter; I suggested that since it was a feast for cold weather, celebrating the turning of the year, that's when we should have it, in June, and all the traditional food would work. Not one of them took that line, they all thought it was a terrible idea. We couldn't go to the beach, they said. What about ice-creams and cold drinks? Far too cold, Christmas should be hot. It was then I realised that Christmas in Australia equals hot weather, and people like it that way. If you're a teenager there's no difference between a tradition as old as you and one as ancient as your most ancient ancestors.

So, what to eat? I favour huge plates of prawns, with lemon juice and rye bread and plenty of cold white wine, eaten in a cool garden. Or oysters, if you can be sure of getting them at the last minute, or any sort of simple seafood that needs no mucking about. Or else this dish, which is easy to make, can be done ahead of time, and is immensely impressive.

GALANTINE

1 good free-range chicken
1 kg chicken minced
200 g chicken livers, cut in chunks
75 g pistachio nuts, whole
1 small onion, finely chopped
1 clove garlic, finely chopped
some green shallots cut in rings
several sprigs thyme (or herbs to suit)
black pepper
grated nutmeg
50 mL dry vermouth, or brandy, or Benedictine
100 g pancetta (not hot)
several tablespoons olive or walnut oil

Have the butcher tunnel-bone the chicken. Mix all the ingredients except the chicken, pancetta and oil together in a bowl to make the stuffing. This should be done some hours or the night before the dish is to be cooked, and 4 or 5 hours should be allowed for the finished dish to cool before serving.

Line the chicken with slices of pancetta. Fill with the stuffing. Close the slit with skewers — a cork-screw shape works well.

Now it can be cooked in a terrine, if you have one large enough, or an oval *gratin* dish. Oil the dish, put in the chicken, rub the skin with more oil.

Cook in a preheated oven at 200°C for 1¼ to 1½ hours. If it starts to brown too much, cover it with paper or foil.

Cool. Lift out on to a plate and surround with the jelly that has formed. It will cut into very elegant slices.

Serve with some interesting greens, tiny un-sweet gherkins, pickled cumquats or cherries at room temperature.

This is really a dish of basic principles. The flavourings of the stuffing can be varied according to taste — and remember the colour, that's mainly what the pistachio nuts are there for. Mushrooms could be added, or strips of chicken breast, or squares of ham to vary the pattern.

A duck could be cooked the same way, with a sharper stuffing, using orange, or perhaps green olives stuffed with almonds.

A genuine galantine is usually poached, wrapped in muslin in simmering stock; but remember it's okay to give up purist habits in Australia these days.

PUDDING

In one respect I'm totally unregenerate; I dote on Christmas pudding. Prawns and Christmas pudding: the old world and the new. Everybody's allowed a bit of ethnic food for the festive season. You can make it ahead of time so that the flavours develop. You do have to cook it for another two hours on the day, which may be a nuisance since the main reason for eating cool food is not to heat up the house, but if you're eating the prawns in the garden this isn't a problem. And Christmas pudding moist and cold is much nicer than cake.

PAU

We're still on course for Compostela, ever south and west. Every day we choose our route, every day we don't cover as much ground as we think we should have, we're too good at stopping and looking. Though we don't do as much of that as we'd like to, either. I still think with regret of the places we didn't manage to see.

Now we're in Pau on the edge of the Pyrénées. It's still hot. We have dinner in a restaurant in a small sloping square, beside a fountain with three lions' heads spouting water in steps down it; there's a slight coolness. The food is indifferent, some good fish soup, but the fish main courses a bit mucky, with rock-like cheesy potatoes on mine. Cosmo has some saffron rice which is pleasant, probably related to that in the enormous *paella* some nearby diners are struggling to eat. Spain is near. There are a lot of late diners and promenaders. It's good fun. But we think sadly of last night and La Bohème, and wish we were there now that we are hungry, after our picnic lunch, and could do it justice.

We drink Jurançon sec, a wine from some eight kilometres distance, very cold and dry, excellent.

The king's favourite wine, says the waiter. No need to ask which king, here. Henry IV, of course.

Henry IV, the Green Gallant, whose statue stands at the prow of the Ile de la Cité, in Paris. Henry IV, the Béarnais, king of Navarre, in whose capital we are sitting, who became king of France, legitimately, but he had to fight for it. Born a stone's throw from here, in the castle, where you can still see the tortoiseshell cradle in which he was laid. Not made of tortoiseshell, but the actual object. His mother, Jeanne, when pregnant with him, went off to war with her husband, to Picardy in the north. When she thought he was just about ready to be born, she came back to Pau: nineteen days in a coach, and over terrible roads. Nineteen days, and her heavily pregnant. I should stop complaining about our little red car. This was in 1553.

While she was in labour she sang Bearnaise songs so that the child wouldn't be a cry-baby, or sour-tempered. And when he was born his grandfather rubbed his lips with garlic and moistened them with wine from a local vineyard: this same Jurançon sec. To make him a true-born son of home. You can see the room where this happened, see the chest-high bed carved with images of French and Navarre kings, sixty-eight of them, suitable motifs for the birth of a king, see the round table and chairs where the family sat while she gave birth. Not genuine, any of these; latter-day copies. Only the cradle and a game of *tric-trac* are the real thing. And an inlaid jewel box. In fact the furnishing of this chateau is mostly pretty frightful, it's the nineteenth-century bourgeois king Louis Philippe's idea of Gothic and Renaissance decor. Plus acres of Gobelins tapestry, very fine if you like that sort of thing. Very fine anyway, really, but not when you're feeling Romanesque. At such moments you can cope with a bit of Gothic, the real thing, but not classical romps in the curious lifelikeness of woven wool. As you walk around you have to keep subtracting the gaudy red and gold from the plain bones of the castle.

Henry's mother was famously tough; one of her contemporaries said the only female thing about her was her genitals. But Jeanne's mother Marguerite, sister of the French king François I, was sung by poets for her beauty, charm, intelligence, goodness. *Marguerites des Marguerites*, they called her, meaning pearl of pearls. (The word margarine has the same root, implying we're eating something precious.) They also called her the Fourth Grace, and the Tenth Muse. She encouraged liberal thinkers, and protected them, religious and otherwise, she admired the *Decameron*, and wrote a series of stories in the same spirit, seventy-two of them, called the *Heptameron*. The castle at Pau was famous for its festivities, its balls, its parties, its dancing, it was one of the great intellectual cities of Europe.

Henry married another Marguerite, another sister of a French king; she was nicknamed Margot. Dumas wrote a novel about her, which was recently turned into a film, with what would have seemed a gratuitous amount of blood if you didn't know the history.

AUTHENTICITY

The real thing, I've said. Genuine; not genuine. Authentic. The chateau is the real thing, it's the actual building that Henry IV was born in, but who knows what ruins it may have fallen into and been restored from. The *tric-trac* board, backgammon, reversing to a chess board, so intricately carved and inlaid it's a piece of jewellery, is interesting because it was handled by him. The bed is not; it may be beautifully carved and handsome and highly valued, but it's not the actual bed that heard the songs of the Béarn sung by the labouring Jeanne, that felt the tremors as she pushed the future king of France into the world. Besides, how can you trust it, in its imitation of the real one? How do you know what liberties may have been taken?

The tortoiseshell cradle is doubly real; it's an actual shell of a tortoise, just as the animal would have lived in it. And it's the actual bed that the newborn child was laid in. So people say. Legend has it. It was a long time ago, 1553. A lot of people would have had to vouch for it in the four-and-a-half centuries since. Were they all to be trusted? Did somebody get it from somebody who said it was the genuine article? Like the grandmother on the top of the Volkswagen, the crocodile in the New York lavatory, you never meet the person who actually saw it, only the friend of the friend who did. Who knows about this tortoiseshell. But that it is the very cradle, we choose to believe. Were we to discover it to be an imitation, it would lose its power.

I've acquired a glossy booklet about the town. On the front it says, *Pau: Ville authentique*. I wonder what this means. Would it be possible for a town not to be authentic, to be a sham, an imitation, a copy? Evidently, if you're thinking of Sovereign Hill at Ballarat, where people are employed to dress up in nineteenth-century clothes and act out the town's original working life as a mining settlement, to give tourists a feel for the original habitation of the town, at the same time as providing its economic viability in the present. It would claim historical accuracy, but it's sanitised, not just physically, emotionally sanitised. Living in Sovereign Hill in the nineteenth century was not the slightest bit like this. You didn't get a salary for doing so. You didn't go home at night, take your costume off and have a hot shower. To call such a town authentic would be a dangerous twist of meaning.

A note from the mayor of Pau repeats the phrase, without much illumination: 'Pau is without doubt an authentic town where vitality, and the quality of life, go hand in hand to the benefit of both its inhabitants and its visitors.'

Perhaps he means it's a town with its reasons for existing in the present, rather than as a theme park marketing its own history. The mayor's first paragraph refers to these things: 'Pau, a town of tolerance; a proud town; renowned for its mild climate, the preservation of its heritage; its rich and lively Béarn culture.' Tolerance is a good thing to mention, since there's been anything but in the past. Marguerite's liberalism was an exception as rare as the pearl she was named for. Her rough daughter

Jeanne got converted to Calvinism so she persecuted Catholics; she was defeated by Charles IX
who punished the Calvinists; he was pushed out by
Jeanne's lieutenant and once again it was the Papists
swinging from the gibbets. And so it went.

Further on the booklet mentions the hyacinth-
coloured evenings of togetherness, but perhaps we
should blame the translation for that. Later it tells us
that whether it's deep blue or light green the Béarn
is always natural.

Natural. There's another word to conjure with.

SAUCE BEARNAISE

This could be a good place to mention the sauce. Its
name suggests that it is a sauce in the manner of the
Béarn but this is in fact a deception. It seems to have
come about in 1830 in the Ile de France, the area
around Paris, invented by a chef of the Pavillon
Henri IV, at St Germain-en-Laye. There are still
various restaurants up and down the country
named after the good King Henry, le Vert Galant,
who was keen on food. His other claim to culinary
fame is his wishing that each one of his subjects
might every Sunday have a chicken in the pot.

I don't often make *sauce béarnaise* these days since
I have become squeamish about that amount of butter, but it is a gorgeous thing. My son used to ask for
it on his birthday, with rare-roasted leg of lamb.

It's one of the emulsion sauces, which make
eggs and fat stick together and turn into something

different; mayonnaise is the oil version. The liaison is delicate. I learned to make it from Edouard de Pomiane the Parisian doctor, son of Polish emigrés, whose books called *Radio Cuisine* after his wireless programmes are my treasured possessions. He says don't make it over boiling water, make it out of boiling water. In other words, dip the pot in the water only briefly, just enough to melt the butter. I won't repeat the recipe here, which is in *Eat My Words*, and anyway any classical one works done this way.

POULET AU POT DOU NOUSTE HENRIC

The idea of cooking a chicken in a pot is to tenderise a tough old hen past its laying days. If one of these doesn't come your way, use a hearty free-range bird. Brown the bird in a large pot, in some olive oil. Add vegetables, an onion, a leek, some turnips, carrots, celery, garlic. Cover with boiling water, bring back to boil, skim.

If it's an old boiler cook for about 3 hours but a young bird should not need much more than an hour; about 40 minutes a kilo. It's important not to overcook. In this case the vegetables may be edible; after 3 hours they won't be, and you'll need to remove them and add fresh to serve with the chicken.

It's good served with a vinaigrette sauce to which you add a soft boiled egg, a small unsweet gherkin, a little sweet onion and some herbs, all finely chopped. The broth can be served first, but I think it is better to

107

cool it and defat. It makes an excellent soup with leek
and potatoes cooked in it, and puréed.

Roasted garlic

Even not thinking of Henry and his infant lips
rubbed with garlic, this is one of my favourite
recipes. You take several heads of garlic, separate
them into cloves, and put them in a saucepan. Just
cover with milk and bring slowly to the boil. Pour off
milk. Put the garlic cloves into a small heavy pot with a
tablespoon of olive oil and a pinch of salt, cover and
cook in a 200°C oven for about half an hour, until tender. Serve with the chicken, as a vegetable. The cloves
of garlic pop out of their skins as you bite into them,
and taste wonderfully nutty and sweet, not at all over-
powering. Excellent with the chicken.

Karaoke

After the disappointing food but pleasant dinner at
Le Dauphin in the Place des Etats in Pau, the
evening becoming more hyacinth by the minute, we
take a little walk. Round a corner, and there's
Henry's castle, floodlit. We lean against its moat
wall and look at it for a while. You can't help won-
dering what his contemporaries would have made
of all this light. All through the centuries everything
must have been so dark, only candles and oil lamps
to illuminate the vast shadowy spaces, which are

still pretty good at defeating the unimaginable candle-power of daylight, so getting up and going to bed with the sun wouldn't have been much help. By candlelight the dim enclosing walls must have seemed as threatening as the dangers they shut out. And then, suddenly, the twentieth century, and such scope for brightness. Such brilliance of illumination. I wish I thought there was a parable there, a symbol, a meaning, but I fear there isn't. Unless in reverse, an irony that with all our brightness of light we see so poorly.

By the moat wall there are tables and chairs belonging to a bar across the road, so we sit down. It's called the Cotton Pub and it's a karaoke bar, the only one in town, it tells us. It has a heavy door, which swings shut. The waiter goes in and out, serving drinks. When the door is open out belts the full force of bad singing amplified to a roar, then, when it's shut again, there's perfect silence. It's surreal, these brief slices of terrible music suddenly cut off by the calm illuminated night of the Renaissance castle.

You have to admire the soundproofing. And presumably it's an example of good heritage management, not allowing noise to pollute this castle and city scape. Or maybe the residents of these handsome old buildings with castle views demanded it.

WINE ALONE

We have another glass of Jurançon sec, this lovely dry and fruity wine. It's good to find a wine that is delicious to drink by itself. French wines often aren't. Not the sort that you can buy in cafés and restaurants by the glass. You understand why people usually have aperitifs, putting cassis in to make a Kir, or drinking vermouths, or pastis, or port. Or whisky is very classy. Wines may go well with food but not be delicious on their own. Whereas in Australia there are a lot of wines that are excellent by themselves, and you can always drink sparkling wines, *faux-champagnes*, when the real thing in France is so expensive that it's only for special occasions. In some ways it's sad that Australian bubblies are perhaps the best cheap wine you can get. What can you drink for a celebration?

When we go to visit Catherine and Etienne, who have a house on the lagoon near Sète, on the Languedoc coast of the Mediterranean, they give us oysters out of the lagoon and wine grown on the property. You stand around on the slatted terrace of the house, Etienne opens the oysters on a big battered tin tray, you bend from the waist and slurp up the oyster and its copious juice (in this part of the world they wouldn't believe that anyone could dream of washing oysters) with mouthfuls of thin dry wine. Not long ago this wine was sold as a whole crop to Noilly Prat just down the coast at Marseillan, to make vermouth; forty spices would be added and all sorts of secret flavourings. But now it is turned into a table wine, of a particular affinity with the oysters grown in the water alongside the grapes. We thought it delicious, and when asked what we wanted for an aperitif, said, Some of this wine of Montpenèdre. But on its own it wasn't particularly nice at all, rather thin, not fruity enough. Our hosts wouldn't consider drinking it like this; they'd add it to blackcurrant liqueur, cassis, or else drink vermouth, or whisky. Less often would they drink pastis, Pernod or Ricard, though they had it in the house.

CHARCUTERIE

The hotel we've found in Pau is in a large square, which gives it its name: the Hotel Gramont. You should always ask to see the room when you arrive at a French hotel, not so much because you might turn it down as because it indicates that you are a person to be considered; you're proclaiming that you won't be fobbed off with just anything. It's particularly important in old hotels which have had to show considerable ingenuity in fitting rooms and baths into existing exiguous spaces. At the Gramont they show us three; we like the cheapest of them, which is very pretty and nattily fitted into the mansard. The floor space isn't very large but the shapes of the ceiling make it seem spacious; it's bright and airy. Not very quiet, the traffic lights five floors down control a lot of very noisy vehicles: frequent buses and trucks. But the bed is excellent. And so is the situation, the closeness to the castle and the centre of town.

We like it so much we decide to stay two nights. On the second day we buy food and picnic in the room, there's a little table, and we lay out the small packets we've bought from a nearby *charcuterie*. It's not a very grand *charcuterie*, indeed a bit depressed, just a few things on offer, as though it doesn't have a very large or discriminating clientele. But it's the only one we can find, on foot; the car's off in some parking organised by the hotel, not close; it takes two people to get it, one to drive the other. Cosmo gets into conversation with the *charcutier* and his wife; they tell him with a kind of tired despair how hard they have to work and still they don't make any money; up at dawn to prepare their wares, still open at eight o'clock and later. Ah, if only they had the money, they'd emigrate, to Australia, perhaps, or Canada, which seems closer. But both impossibly distant; so hard as they work, they barely survive, there's no chance of their ever making enough money to move.

We buy some salads, *céleri rémoulade* and carrot, an excellent *tartare de saumon*, some *brandade de morue*, a dish of salt cod which is truly wonderful. And *jambon de Bayonne*, the local ham, a raw ham like a prosciutto which the wife cuts in thick juicy slices. With some cheese, the local Pyrénées, which is made of a mixture of cow's and sheep's milk, a firm pale slightly slippery cheese.

And some Jurançon sec, of course; the *charcutier* sells wine too. Not cold, it's almost impossible to buy cold wine, even in Paris. Sometimes a Nicolas shop would have perhaps several bottles of Muscadet chilled, but that was lucky. The *charcutier* offers to put our wine in his refrigerator; we can come back in half an hour and collect it.

The picnic is not exactly an economical exercise; buying this food costs just about as much as a modest restaurant meal. It's the perennial French mystery, how well one can eat in restaurants for how little, compared with what the raw materials cost.

The things we buy are all very good; we've chosen them carefully. There were some other salads, but they looked tired, as though they'd sat there for too long. I imagine the couple staring hopelessly at them, wishing that somebody would buy them, take them off their hands, slowly coming to terms with the fact of having to throw them away. Possibly not doing this soon enough, ruining their business by selling faded food. I remember my father who at the time I was born kept a general shop. He'd tell how he'd go to the market and buy lettuces, lovely crisp fresh lettuces, and put them out, and nobody would buy them, and they'd sit there, and eventually a customer would come in, wanting a lettuce, and stare at them and say, hmm, they look a bit wilted, don't they, and not buy one. It would break your heart, said my father. They sold that shop when I was two, because it was no life for a family, they'd open at six in the morning to catch the early workers, and stay open till eleven at night, hoping for somebody coming home from the pictures. My father reckoned that if they'd kept it they'd have made a fortune, in the late 1940s, when business flourished and the baby boomers were being born, but what a terrible life it would have been.

I used to wonder what it would be like to be the daughter of a rich man, but couldn't somehow imagine it.

CELERI REMOULADE

This is a salad of celeriac or celery root (*céleri-rave*), dressed with a very mustardy sauce, which is what the *rémoulade* part means.

Take a celery root, peel it, and grate it very finely, in a food processor or a vegetable mill, or even by hand against a metal grater — I've done this in tool-less kitchens, and it works. Make a dressing by putting a tablespoon of Dijon mustard in a bowl and adding 1 shallow dessertspoon wine vinegar. Beat using a small balloon whisk. Gradually add oil, much as for mayonnaise, and you should get a liaison; it won't be as stable as a mayonnaise, and if it separates or doesn't ever take don't worry, give it a final whip and stir in the grated vegetable. Add pepper, and salt if desired, stir well.

CARROT SALAD

I give this because it's such a good salad and often made so badly. Carrot is a sweet vegetable and shouldn't have sugar added, or honey, or even raisins, as is so often done.

Grate some carrots finely, as for celeriac. Make a vinaigrette of oil and vinegar, adding some finely chopped sweet onion — half a large onion would be plenty, a quarter would do. A lot of chives would be pretty. Toss well.

It's the absolute simplicity of these two salads that makes them so good.

TARTARE DE SAUMON

This is an imitation using fish of a steak tartare.

Cut 300 g of very fresh salmon or salmon trout into small dice. Mix 1 tablespoon olive oil, 1 teaspoon wine vinegar, 1 egg yolk. Finely chop and add 1 teaspoon small capers, 1 tablespoon cornichons (small, unsweet gherkins), 2 anchovy fillets, 3 spring onions. Mix in 1 teaspoon wasabi paste and a little pepper. Stir gently.

This can be eaten in various ways, for instance with some rye bread. I like to serve it in leaves of witloof (Belgian endive): trim the root and pull the leaves away, spoon a little of the mixture into the leafy end. The contrast of the slightly bitter crisp witloof and the rich salmon is very good. It's very tidy to eat so it makes good party food.

Plenty for six at dinner, or more for a party.

PYRENEES

One of the famous landmarks of Pau is the boulevard des Pyrénées, Napoleon's idea, to build a great terrace along the edge of the city, out over the valley, a place of promenade from which there is a marvellous view of the mountains. In clear weather, that is. This hot weather is heavy, although the sun shines and so hotly that you'd rather not walk about in it. The air is thick. We read the orientation table, pointing out what famous peaks may be seen, we look at glossy photographs of their massive snowy grandeur, but cannot see even a shadowy outline of them. Not until days later, as we are about to leave the region of the Pyrénées behind, do we suddenly catch a glimpse of peaks so high, so close, that we realise we have not at all understood the country we have been passing through.

Agatha Christie writes in her autobiography of going to live in Pau when she was about six, in the 1890s; her parents were feeling a bit strapped for money so they rented out their house in Torquay complete with servants and came to live in Pau, in a hotel, which was cheaper than living in England. The hotel must have been on this terrace, because she mentions her dreadful disappointment; she expected to see great mountains but could only make out, in the distance, a row of small teeth.

THE ENGLISH

Pau has always been popular with the English, or at least since the Romantic period. There's still a direct flight from London during the season. They like the climate. And presumably it was on their behalf that fox-hunting was organised; people can hire horses and follow the hunt through the forest. So says my elderly guidebook, which dates from Cosmo's days with the natural gas installations; I wonder if you still can. The modern brochure makes more of the 140-year-old golf course, the oldest on the continent, laid out in the British tradition, as well as the Royal Golf Club and the Scottish Golf Club, set among vineyards and hillocks. And the casino, and the performing arts festivals, and the *son et lumière* at the end of the hyacinth evenings. So perhaps fox-hunting is a thing of the past.

BREAKFAST

Two days in Pau have proved quite restful. We're up early and zipping unbreakfasted down the motor-way, which would take us to Bayonne, but we turn south and begin our journey through the Pyrénées, stopping at the first likely café. On the outskirts of a town called Salies-de-Béarn, some sixty kilometres from Pau. It's a *relais*, a stage, of the kind that the stage coach would have stopped at: restaurant, café, service station, some rooms.

It's just opening. Yes, we can have coffee. Croissants? No, she has no croissants ... ah, but wait. Yes, croissants. A young man rushes off in a small car. We sit on the terrace in the early morning coolness. The young man comes back. The crois-sants are hot and fresh from a bakery in the town. Coffee and croissants and the bright morning air: it's a wonderful breakfast.

When we go inside to the lavatory, through the

main café, we discover some locals set up at a table
in the window looking out over a flowery garden.
Farmers, or peasants perhaps, agricultural workers
anyway, in the vivid blue heavy cotton clothes that
workmen in France wear. On the table is a litre
bottle of red wine, a large bread, and a pot of some
country pâté. It looks delicious. Madame says this is
a light breakfast, sometimes she has to cook. We've
put in a good morning ourselves, we can see the
pleasure of it.

GERANIUMS

It's time I mentioned the geraniums. The whole of
France is blooming with geraniums; roses sometimes, and petunias occasionally, but mainly geraniums, red ones, flowering against grey stone walls.
We have begun to use them like a star system, for
grading: good geraniums; so-so; pretty poor; none.
An establishment without decent geraniums is not
the kind of place you'd want to go to. The evidence
it offers of not caring is too blatant. And there are so
many good geraniums, why go to a place where
they're only so-so? The geraniums of this glorified
garage where we're breakfasting count as good.
They're so heavily in flower, not like mine at home,
where I'm lucky if I get one or two blooms; these
spray all over the place.

And it's not just restaurants and cafés, it's private
houses. No village is too small, too plain, too poor;
always there is this gorgeous frolic of colour to

gladden the eye. And the heart, for those who are depressed do not cultivate geraniums in pots and hanging baskets, of plastic, terracotta, iron, in old saucepans, tubs, oilcans, in stone troughs that might have been a sarcophagus in Gallo-Roman times. Not caring if they make narrow streets narrower. Marking the absence of depression: moral, spiritual, not just financial. Ground-down poverty does not buy flowers. Bare subsistence has neither money nor energy to decorate itself.

In some towns there is a poster in the bakery window, or in the Syndicat d'Initiative, with a bunch of painted flowers and the words: *Fleurissons nos villes*. How to translate ... Let us make our towns flower ... Let us deck our towns with flowers ... Let us bring them into bloom. And in there is the idea of flourishing, of prospering.

That is the message of these geraniums blossoming in every available corner, ledge, window-sill: they say we are prosperous. We are not just surviving, not just subsisting, we are flowering.

LEGENDS

We don't actually go into Salies-de-Béarn, a place known for its waters, which are salty and good for women and children and bones; you can see the salt in the name. Instead we make for Sauveterre-de-Béarn, a postcard pretty place, built on an escarpment above a river. The green fields, the willows, the yellow sunshine together produce a kind of tremulous green-gold light that breathes tranquil-lity. Across the river is a bridge, part of a bridge, with towers, and a legend.

1170. Sancie, widow of Gaston V of Béarn, is accused of murdering her child, born posthumously. She is subjected to the judgement of God. Ordered by her own brother, the king of Navarre. This is how God's judgement will show itself: her wrists and ankles are tied and she is thrown into the river from the top of one of the towers of the fortified bridge. God chooses to save her, or not. The word for this river is *gave*, which means a mountain torrent, though it looks lazy enough on this summer morn-ing. Anyway, some 800 years ago the river's current washed her up on the bank, whole and undrowned. Obviously she's innocent. She's reinstated: goes back to being noblewoman, widow, king's sister. All her worldly dues are repaid her.

Just as well her accusers didn't think she was a witch; the water casting her up like that might have been construed as a sign that she was guilty, as in the old ducking test: float and you're guilty, sink and you're innocent.

It's high, the fortified bridge. I wonder in what season she was subjected to this judgement of God. God in this case owing much to the interpretation of man. I like to think of there being a special circle in hell which God reserves for those who claim their own chosen cruel judgements are His. Had it been winter she might have been less lucky; the moun-tain torrent would be icy, and in spring snow-fed. Death comes in seconds in such cold waters.

Though God doubtless could have dealt with that, sending not just a current but a warm one to cast her up on the bank. Perhaps it was summer, but even in summer that bound fall through the quivering light-filled air would have been full of terror. You can hear her scream: faint across space and time, yet still the air trembles with it.

This is what we are here for: the reverberation of a scream down the centuries. So, just for a moment, the past is now; a woman is thrown plummeting from a bridge, the water does not drown her. Bloody stories, with or without happy endings, the grand old themes of love and death, that's what we're here for.

WALLED CITY

And wars, or the stony memories of them. We arrive in the middle of the day at St-Jean-Pied-de-Port, whose name describes it: St John at the foot of the pass, *port* here meaning not the same as the English word but mountain pass. It's got an old town, which is surrounded by ramparts, the high town, it is called, *ville haute*, as so often, because it is strategically placed for military purposes, not for the ease of its inhabitants. There are a lot of brightly dressed sightseers struggling up its steep streets in the hot sunlight. You can't take your car in unless you live there. The ramparts of this high town are fifteenth century, and there are some more on the other side of the river that are seventeenth century.

St-Jean-Pied-de-Port, being the last stop before Spain, used to be a great meeting place for pilgrims. There were a lot of hospices to look after them, everything was organised, down to a tourist guide-book with not very complimentary remarks about the manners of the locals and their mentality. The arrival of pilgrims was a signal for festivity; bells rang, priests recited prayers, children ran along beside, townsfolk offered provisions, a procession formed, singing. Suddenly a living forest is climbing into the mountains, all the pilgrims carrying a cross of foliage, which they've made themselves and will set down on the pass.

But as time passed beggars (annoying the local poor, who didn't like this invasion of their territory) and adventurers, tricksters, a kind of medieval car-petbagger, mixed in with the pilgrims and caused disturbances. In the steep street you can see the fourteenth-century Bishops' Prison where such offenders were held. By the sixteenth century true pilgrims were rare. And they needed permits from the king and their parish priest.

Now the visitors to St-Jean-Pied-de-Port are straight out holiday-makers. Here for the sights, for-tified towns and old buildings adding special inter-est to the summer vacation. Local authorities know this; everywhere there are spanking-fresh signs pointing to abbeys, churches, towers, bridges. Here travellers are offered fishing as well. And mountain scenery. And walks. The town is full of good humour as they saunter about, buying souvenirs, the local Basque embroidery, or pottery, or things which simply say they are a souvenir of this or whatever place they are bought in. Browsing in the wineshop for some local vintages: Irouleguy is a famous one; its name very Basque, which is one of those orphan languages that don't seem to have any parents or siblings, nobody knows whence they came. Photographing the old bridge, and the fortified church which forms part of the ramparts, and the ancient houses which border the River Nive. Deciding what to do about lunch.

A picnic? Some slices of local raw ham, with bread and cheese and fruit? A sandwich? Some hot cheesy pastry thing?

On the other side of the road is a serious-looking establishment, the usual café-restaurant-hotel. It has a terrace right on the bank of the Nive, shady, hung with geraniums. Very good geraniums. And tables with white cloths, and round tall glasses that sparkle in the cool light under the trees. Waiters of style and bustle, in the manner of the old school. We'll just go and read the menu. Of the Hotel Central on the bank of the Nive.

Well, it has chicken *Basquaise*. Ah, we must try this, it may be our only chance. We eat chicken *Basquaise* at home a lot. Last time we were in France we got some of the necessary pimento, the red pepper spice, like paprika but more piquant, from a shop specialising in Basque products. It will be good to try it on the spot. The genuine article. Authentic.

We get into conversation with the waiter. Where can we buy some of the red pepper spice? Whereabouts in the town is the shop that will sell it to us? *Pardon*? he says. The red pepper spice, the *poivre rouge*, the *piment*, for seasoning chicken *Basquaise*? He doesn't know, he can't help us. There will be a harvest of *piments rouges*, they grow on the fields round the town, but not yet, it's not the right season. The spice? He brings a bottle of some sinister-looking proprietary sauce. Is this what we mean? The restaurant doesn't use it, certainly not, but maybe we (he doesn't say, being foreigners, but we understand it) would consider it a good idea.

When we taste the chicken we realise why communication has been difficult. The dish is pleasant, chicken stewed with fresh red capsicum, some tomato and such, but there's no spice, no piquancy, it's quite bland. The waiter doesn't know what we're talking about because they aren't using it, here.

This raises the question of authenticity, yet again. Is it our dish, made from reading serious books on the matter? Claiming the actual recipes of informed people? Or the locally made dish in a decent bourgeois hotel?

We try chicken *Basquaise* again later. It's bland again. In Biarritz I buy a recipe-postcard of it, to send to Lucy, who's the chicken *Basquaise* specialist in our house. It reads pretty blandly too. Mind you, recipe-postcards are mostly hopeless; a good idea but rarely is there anything you'd want to make, not that the basic dish is bad, it's the particular cute tourist version. Usually the equivalent of the gimcrack souvenir, not the real thing.

Here's Lucy's recipe. Authentic? Who knows. It's very good.

Chicken *Basquaise*

 8 pieces chicken (preferably boneless thigh pieces, or breast)
2 large onions chopped roughly
2 slices ham (or pancetta or prosciutto) chopped in squares
1 green pepper chopped roughly
1 red pepper ditto
2 tins tomatoes
1/2 teaspoon (generous) pimento

Use a large frying-pan or copper sauté pan. Melt onion in several tablespoons of olive oil. Add, in this order, ham (cook only slightly), chicken pieces (brown these), green and red pepper, tomatoes. Put the lid on the pan and let the mixture soften. Add the pimento about 15 minutes later and leave with lid on to simmer for the next 15–20 minutes until chicken is tender and peppers are soft.

There is often enough sauce left over to make a lunch of eggs. Heat sauce, break in eggs, and cook until set.

Serves four.

Capsicum

Of course one of the things which makes this chicken a Basque dish is raw ham. And there certainly is a spice, called *pimenton*, which Tom Stobart's *Cook's Encyclopaedia* describes as the Spanish equivalent of paprika, and very important: used in sausages like *chorizo*, and in *escabèche* of fish, where it preserves as well as flavours. It's sold loose in Spanish markets, and is dark vermilion in colour, or else tomato red.

This is definitely what I was looking for in St-Jean-Pied-de-Port, what I bought in Paris. Calling it the Spanish equivalent of paprika is a bit sloppy; it's hotter, and if you put too much in you'll end up with a dish that burns the tongue.

In fact these are both varieties of capsicum, which can be mild and sweet, or pungent and fiery hot, and degrees in between. There's a gamut of them, from chilli at one end to paprika at the other; there's a scale of hotness that includes varying degrees of chilli, cayenne pepper, and this Spanish *pimenton*.

So the spice is real. It's the genuine article. It just doesn't seem to be used in cooking chicken.

Once, in my purist youth, I'd have accepted that. Made the dish as the locals did. Just as, when Elizabeth David said *quiche lorraine* never had cheese in it, I never made it with cheese (and very good it is without). But now I don't care. The whole country I live in doesn't care, either. We live in a melting pot. Things get mixed up. Chicken *Basquaise* tastes better with *pimenton*. That's enough.

CHILLI

Or chili. Or chilly.

Look at this for a list: *cascabel, chilaca, guajilo, guero, habanearo, jalapeno, poblano, serrano, mulato, pasado, ancho, chipotle* ...

All the names of different kinds of chilli. Altogether there are two hundred. They have different colours and levels of hotness and intensities of flavour, and if you know about them they are not at all interchangeable. In Mexico, Spain, South America, and India, you select them for your purpose. The recipes in the book, *Like Water for Chocolate*, specify particular kinds of chilli: about a hundred are available in Mexico. They may be pea-sized or thirty centimetres long. Chillis are the flavouring above all used by poor people the world over, since they make almost anything palatable, says Stobart. But their use is highly sophisticated.

People who begin to eat chilli tend to want more and more. It's not the tastebuds that register it, but pain receptors in the mouth that are stimulated by the chemical capsicain it contains. Some people think that since eating chilli causes us to feel pain, the body releases endorphins, which create euphoria, and so we get addicted not to the flavour but to the euphoria. I've heard that soda water has the same effect.

HARISSA

While we're on the subject of chillies we could consider harissa, the sauce used with couscous. It is a dish of the Arabs at home in North Africa, not Spanish Arab. A proper couscous is made by steaming the grain in a vessel just for this purpose, above a simmering chicken or lamb stew. But you can get instant couscous which works rather well; follow the directions on the packet. It is best made with chicken stock. I like to serve couscous with a salad of roasted vegetables and a harissa-style sauce.

Prepare a collection of vegetables — cherry tomatoes, courgettes, aubergines, onions, peppers, spring onions. Slice them into strips or squares, toss them in several tablespoons of olive oil mixed with 3 cloves of garlic and some basil leaves, and roast in a 175°C oven for 30–40 minutes.

Place the couscous in a large shallow dish and arrange the vegetables over the top. Serve with a harissa-style sauce.

HARISSA-STYLE SAUCE
1/2 cup olive oil
1 teaspoon sambal oelek (a good way to use chillies — it is rather hot, use less, or more, according to taste)
2 tablespoons ground cumin
2 heaped tablespoons tomato purée (*not* paste)
juice of 2 lemons, or limes

Mix ingredients well together.

FISH

The terrace where we're sitting to have our lunch juts out over the river a little, just downstream from a bridge. People keep stopping on this bridge, looking down into the water, pointing. Here the river is shallow, limpid, with long thin islands of gravel separating it into streams. I lean out over our balustrade to see what it is the people on the bridge are looking at. There, in the water, is an enormous trout, hanging lazily in the shallow stream, nose to the current. Leading an idyllic trout life, teasing the audience with its plumpness.

MOUNTAIN PASSES

There are a number of roads through the Pyrénées, not very many. In the heyday of the pilgrims there were three, and still are; the route we are taking, to Puente la Reina where they all meet, will pass through Roncevaux, and there's another story.

Twelve hundred years old, this one: 778, and the Emperor Charlemagne has captured nearly all of Spain from the Saracens. Only Saragossa remains. The Saracen king offers terms, involving a French withdrawal, terms which are in fact treacherous, though Charlemagne's council can't agree on this Moorish perfidy. Roland, his most glorious knight, is against accepting the offer, Ganelon in favour of it; Ganelon prevails. Roland is in charge of the retreating army. Ganelon turns traitor, he betrays Roland and the rearguard of the army. This consists of 20 000 men, crossing the Pyrénées; in the pass at Roncevaux they are surrounded by 400 000 Saracens. Oliver the beloved companion-in-arms of Roland urges him to sound his horn and call back

the main body of the army. But Roland refuses. The
battle is bitter and bloody, the knights, the great
peers of France, fight like the heroes they are, but
gradually their army is destroyed. When at last only
sixty men remain alive, Roland sounds his horn, his
ivory oliphant, but it is too late. There are four men
left, wounded to death.

Roland puts the horn to his mouth and clenches
it firmly and with great force sounds on it. High
are the peaks and the voice of the horn is long.
Over thirty great leagues they hear it echo.
Charles hears it, and all his companies. Says the
king, Our men are in battle. Ganelon disagrees: If
another had said this, he would be a liar, he tells
the king.

Count Roland sounds the horn with pain and
dolour and great toil. The bright blood springs
from his mouth, and the temple of his brain is
burst with it. The sound of the horn carries a
mighty distance; it reaches Charles on his way
through the mountain passes.

Roland and Oliver, who began as enemies but
fought themselves into the most famous of knightly
friendships, take their farewell of one another and
prepare for death. Roland tries to break his sword
Durendel by smiting a rock with it, but only suc-
ceeds in opening up a great breach.

Roland strikes upon a dark grey rock. He chops
down more of it than I can describe, the sword

grates, but it does not shatter, does not break, but rather rebounds against the sky. When the Count sees that he will never break it, he laments gently to himself, Ah Durendel, how beautiful you are, and holy; in your gilded pommel there are many relics: St Peter's tooth and the blood of St Basil, hair from my lord St Denis, and a piece of the robe of the holy Mary. It is not right that pagans should hold you. You must be served by Christians.

Roland lies down upon his sword, he wants to die with it close to him. He offers up his mind to God, he makes his confession, and God receives it; the heavens open and angels and cherubim, St Michael and St Gabriel, bear away the soul of the Count to Paradise.

You can still see the great breach that Durendel made in the rock at Roncevaux; and also at Gavarnie, more than 100 kilometres away: you can take your pick as to which is the genuine one.

As for Durendel, it is evidently a kind of portable pilgrimage; no need to travel to the places of holy relics, Roland carries them with him.

Charlemagne and his army arrive to find Roland and Oliver dead. They set about avenging them; they rout the Saracens and take Saragossa. In order to give him enough daylight to capture the infidel, God answers Charlemagne's prayer and stops the sun.

For Charlemagne God made a great miracle, for the sun has stood still in its tracks. The pagans are fleeing and the Francs are pursuing them. In the valley of shadows they overtake them. They pursue them fiercely on toward Saragossa and slay them with powerful blows.

These words are from *The Song of Roland*. This particular story was a favourite with the pilgrims; you can understand why. The poetry in Old French makes the heart swell even when you don't understand it; there is glory in its cadences, and even a basic English translation is powerful. The pilgrims entertained themselves with this *Chanson de Geste*, this chronicle of heroic exploits, this tale of Moor fighting, as they made their way through the countryside in which it happened. Though the telling is four centuries younger.

The authors of the *Chansons de Geste* are not known, but it is thought they may have been monks in monasteries along the pilgrim way, who noted down good stories about their own places, in order to get pilgrims to stop there — like television commercials designed to attract tourists. Except they were marvellous poets.

Relic stealing was another way of enhancing your reputation as a stage worth the visit or even a detour. But it's the *Chansons de Geste* that remain, some eighty of them.

So the pilgrims repeated these stories on their travels. As do we, leaving St-Jean-Pied-de-Port basking in its summer holiday sun, the car climbing up steepening roads. Crossing the border, which is deserted, nobody to stamp our passports or check our visas — my visa, Cosmo being a New Zealander doesn't have to have one. The sun disappears, we are driving through a mist which hangs in droplets, the air is dense and silenced, save for faint liquid drippings from the trees and the noise of our puny labouring engine. The road narrows, it switches back on itself, it climbs up the mountain in a series of acute zigzags. We crawl up, sticking to the edge, the silence is broken by the hurtle of lorries, this is the only route for the Europe lorries too, travelling at downhill speed and grabbing both sides of the road. In between the juggernauts, in the silence, we think of Roland and the painful note of his horn sounding too late to save him from the slaughtering Moors.

And we think of the true story: Charlemagne in Spain, certainly, but at the request of two Moorish emirs having a fight with a third. Capturing Pamplona and Saragossa possibly, then having to go home to quell an uprising among his own people. This is always a problem with wars, what happens at home while you are away. The natives getting restless. The Basques, then as now pursuing their own interests, surprised the retreating army and wiped it out. It didn't need many of them to do this, they could pick off the soldiers one by one in the narrow defile of the mountain pass, crushing them with chunks of rock and ripped-up trees that they rolled down the cliffs.

This is the historical as opposed to the heroic narrative. The Basques have a heroic one, too, *The Poem of Bernardo del Carpio*, the story of the young cham-

pion who avenges the violation of Spanish soil by
the French army.

PANTHERS

You might think that the Middle Ages and the days
of heroic narrative are long dead and never did
have any life in Australia, but I'm not sure that this
is true.

I went to one of those several-day meetings that
are held in a hotel, which offers conference facilities
and guest accommodation in a package; the place
was the Panthers Motor Inn and Leagues Club, at
Penrith. The idea was to have an experience of
Western Sydney which was very interesting too but
for me there was more than that. The Panthers Motor
Inn is named for the local football team and it is as
medieval a set-up as I have seen. It is combined with
the Panthers Leagues Club which is home to the
mighty Penrith Panthers: the whole edifice is created
by this small band of, you can only call them,
knights, whose glory is their strength, whose legend
is their invincibility, whose prowess carries their
name throughout the land. Football is their game,
rather than shaking swords at one another, but the
rules aren't all that different. The club is a court like
Charlemagne's or Arthur's; the knights sally forth
from home ground to do battle, or hold tournaments
and invite their foes on to their own territory.

The club/court has its own banners, its insignias,
its coats of arms. Its mottos, slogans, war cries. The

set of buildings which houses it is enormous, it
occupies the horizon, it is feudal in its scope, and
impregnable in its way. Many serfs are in thrall to it.
It takes money from them, by means of its poker
machines, but in return for their fealty it is kind. It is
a place of shelter and of pastimes, always open. It is
a mighty employer, and is benevolent. It is the castle
as city, it could withstand a siege, everything is
within it. And if there is within it a sense of belea-
guerment — well, I'm not sure what meaning to
draw from the pun.

For many people, to be obliged to leave would
be to be bereft; they would feel that where life was
had cast them out. The footballers themselves, the
knights, the heroes, are rarely to be seen, but their
glory is omnipresent, a matter of reverence and awe,
the necessary energy of the structure. Which has its
own particular attention to detail. Like the Ironbark
Restaurant, containing unreal gum trees with koalas
in them that wave, and chooks that flap from tin
roofs. Not alive of course, a kind of toy, mechanical.

I don't know what to say about the role of women
in all this. It's as tightly defined as in courtly love,
and as marginal, but probably less interesting.

RONCEVAUX

By the time we arrive at Roncevaux we're cold and
shivering and full of unease. Something has got on
our nerves. Ancient slaughters, or today's Euro-
lorries? There's certainly a great sense of doom in

the dense air and the weeping trees. The monastery isn't much better. It feels neglected. It has vast grey walls and bluish zinc roofs. There are a few young people about, kids, who seem to be part of some scheme for occupying jobless youth; they have a glum and restless air, they horse about, but not hopefully. There's a large shop, with masses of pilgrim souvenirs and some local food; it's evidently for tourists but the girls behind the counter speak only Spanish, except for one who has a bit of French.

There's a cloister, calm as cloisters always are, but sad. The mist weeping. The rest of the place has the rather desperate idle restlessness of the kids, as though it's waiting for something to happen, and fears nothing will, that past treacheries are all there'll ever be. And old poems that were only true in people's minds.

We think with regret of St-Jean-Pied-de-Port, living so cheerfully in its present. Its past is there, weighty as the walls of its fortified city, cosseted and cared for, but its citizens tread lightly on its ancient stones.

SPAIN

We still haven't seen the Pyrénées. Maybe that's what's unnerved us, crossing these massive looming mountains with never a sight of a peak. The map tells us we are leaving them behind, driving down to foothills, into the sunshine again and the hot yellow fields of Spain. The next town is Pamplona, it looks a good place to stop. It's famous for the running of its bulls; every year in July the bulls for the evening's fight are let loose, at eight in the morning, to gallop through the streets to the arena. The young men of the town jump into the street and run in front of them. The bulls are large, angry, full of energy; the brave young men, the foolhardy young men, are in genuine and authentic danger from their horns. World television comes and photographs it; somebody usually gets hurt, sometimes killed. It's real Hemingway stuff. Hemingway loved Pamplona.

I'm navigating, as usual. Cross-referencing the *Michelin* green guide against *Let's Go Spain*. We forgot to find out before we left France what the peseta is worth. This makes our usual financial judgement unworkable. We can get pesetas out of bank machines, but have no way of knowing whether they're four to a dollar like the French franc or a thousand to a dollar like the Italian lira. Well, that's an exaggeration; the girl in the shop at Roncevaux, perhaps I should say Roncesvalles now, told us she thought they were probably about twenty-five to the franc. But that's rather vague.

I'm working on getting us a hotel in the old town. The trouble with old towns is that all the streets are one way, but this is never marked on maps. I can find the street on the map and in its solid grey stone and cobbled reality, but we can't get into it. We go round a few times. The street we want is there, just there. Going down one block doesn't help. The traffic has no patience with us. Nor do fierce-looking policemen. In France some policemen held up the traffic so we could do an illegal U-turn, when we got lost in Melun, but here they just want us out of the way. Well, it is evening, promenade time, the whole town is out. When we find ourselves within sight of another hotel altogether we're overcome with relief; it's biggish and grandish and more pesetas than the one we had in mind, but it's here. At least we're still in the old town.

The Hotel Maisonnave. A fine thirties building. Highly bourgeois. No English spoken, but they can manage a bit of French. We're discovering we don't know as much Spanish as we thought. We ask to see the room. It's okay. Dull, but quiet. A bed, a chair, a dressing-table. No grace, no frills. The usual. The bathroom looks original, mildly grand. It floods.

The old town has narrow streets and crowds of these promenading people. Mostly young, good-looking in the take-it-or-leave-it way of the young everywhere. They remind Cosmo of the Uni Bar at home. Pamplona is the seat of a large private university. We sit in the main square and drink a glass of wine. We know the thing to do in Spain is eat *tapas*, and so we will, but we'll have a glass of wine first, ordered from a waiter. It seems cheap. We've got plenty of pesetas from a bank machine, but are still not sure what they're worth. We find a Change, but it's closed, and has taken down its sign with currency values.

The *tapas* bars are crowded, with people who are so at home in them that we feel clumsy about trying. This is being quite salutary. We realise how easy France is for us, how we know the way things work. The rituals of cafés, the conventions of restaurants. And Cosmo speaking the language like a native; the French think he's a native from somewhere else, they know he's not a local, his accent isn't that perfect, but they don't suppose him to be a foreigner. Everybody knows I'm a foreigner, but at least I can communicate. Here we can't, none of our languages work. Nobody speaks English. And the customs, the habitudes, we are uncertain of. Moreover there aren't any other foreigners. Everybody seems to be a native. But we will try a *tapas* bar. After we've had a glass of wine. *Vino tinto* is red wine. *Rioja*. The speeding waiter smiles. Good. And it is, very good wine.

We promenade a little, then find a place that doesn't seem too full. We need a bit of patience, on their part, I mean. Being a bit empty we'd normally think a bad sign in a café; here it seems a good place to start. We point at little goodies, and they come, on plates, with forks. Some excellent little bready things, that taste like egg sandwiches, and some small meaty parcels, delicious.

Suddenly the place fills up. People crowd and push. We must have struck a lull. We are cast in the role of observers here. We have no part in this life, we can only watch it. All these lives full of energetic conversation and we can know nothing of them. As a novelist I know I am a voyeur, but here I am a *voyeur manqué*. A failed voyeur. It's an interesting situation.

We promenade some more. We've seen the church of St Saturnin several times now. These are the streets where the bulls run; they board them up while it's happening, then afterwards it's business as normal. Is it always this busy? It's Saturday night, maybe on other days it's quieter. The whole town seems to be out and it's all young and prosperous. An amazing life of walking and conversation, and everybody greatly caught up in the excitement of it. Finally we go into a restaurant, a big bright place, not intimidating.

We order prawns with garlic. A number of young people have come in and are eating mixed plates, *platos*, a whole lot of different things all served on the one dish. I hadn't liked the sound of them much, on the menu, but they do seem to be the thing to have. If I'm going to eat a lot I like it to come in small courses, not all piled together.

The garlic prawns take me back to my youth, when this dish was the height of sophistication. They taste good. It's a pity that fashion in Australia makes us lose perfectly okay dishes, like chicken Kiev done properly; it's either debased into ready prepared food or else not done at all. Though Gay Bilson cooked it at a dinner for the announcement of one of the Geraldine Pascall Awards, in a meal that to me deliberately evoked the beginnings of fine dining, in the days of our culinary innocence. Chicken Kiev, followed by strawberries Romanoff. And of course, in her hands, delicious.

Back at the hotel there's a wedding going on. It was before we left. A huge party in a sort of basement banqueting hall. The noise is tremendous. The door opens and lets out the sound, like the karaoke bar, but when it's shut it's still very loud. You can see it's being a celebration to remember. In a hazy way.

Breakfast is included in the cost of the hotel so of course we have it. It's a spread: cold meats, fruits, croissants, eggs, bacon, pastries, orange juice, coffee. The dining-room is full of affluent Spaniards tucking in. So are we. It's a change from the *grand crème*, the cup of strong milky espresso, and the croissant we are in the habit of having. It should set us up for the day.

We drive round the city a bit. Some policemen get very agitated. They seem to suspect us of wicked intent. I don't know how you're supposed to know you're not allowed to enter these streets. Are they one-way, or merely off limits? Is it some Sunday thing? All available roads seem to lead to the same circuit, so we give up trying to find the bull ring and depart for Puente la Reina. The driver is very keen that I stop trying to learn how to navigate incomprehensible traffic. Especially as mine is the theory, his is the practice.

MEETING PLACE

The threads of the pilgrimage routes that began in Paris, Vézelay, Le Puy, Arles, already ravelled into these towns from England, Germany, East Europe, Scandinavia, cross the Pyrénées and form into a knot at Puente la Reina; after that, there's the single strand of the journey across Spain. Puente la Reina: Queen's Bridge. There really is a bridge. A steep arch of a kind called a donkey's back. It's carried on four wide arches supported on buttresses that are themselves pierced with tall thin arches. Plain, elegant, very beautiful. It was built in the eleventh century.

Today a lot of roads have led to Puente la Reina: there's a grand canoe race. We stand on the newish road bridge and watch crowds of these small craft lining up in the water. Both bridges are lined with families and friends of the competitors. Everybody is dressed in bright colours. Holidays and sport equal primary colours. There's a lot of excitement and loud barracking. I take a photo: the ancient slope of the bridge with its towered gateway, in lemony grey stone, lined with cheering spectators, and the coloured canoes shooting through the water under it. A nice juxtaposition. History and daily life. The tourist can only look on with envy; these noisy barrackers jumping up and down and waving their arms own the bridge in a way the tourist never can, they own it by ignoring it, as an idea if not as an object, by taking it for granted, by using it for their own purposes. The tourists marvel at it, while the locals forget about it.

The thing about coming from the new world is that you can never forget about history. Every time I go past the Landsdowne bridge near Liverpool, on the outskirts of Sydney, a bridge which is also a gracious stone arch, though much smaller, and considerably younger, I notice it, its local golden sandstone, I remember it was built by convicts, and that it was one of Macquarie's constructions, resembling certain Tasmanian bridges, and important to the developing colony. I can never take it for granted as a means of crossing a river.

Puente la Reina is famous for the golden-coloured stone and brick of its houses, and the carved wooden beams that support their roofs. In the narrow main street that leads to the bridge (not the wide main road with cafés and shops that crosses the river on the road bridge, this is quiet, secret almost) some restoration work has been going on, the houses are beginning to be in elegant order, with iron balconies and some excellent geraniums. Also in this street is the church of St James, with a highly gilded statue of the saint bearing staff and cockle-shell hat. A townswoman comes in and seems to be very keen that we photograph him, so we do. Of course, she may have been talking about something quite different.

On the edge of the town is the church of the Crucifix; this is the one with the ancient hospice where we see our modern proud pilgrims with the station-wagon. The church is famous for its Y-shaped Christ on the Cross, a thin lifelike figure, with scourge marks and nail holes. It would have been brought from Germany — you can tell by the particular expressionist style — by a fourteenth-century pilgrim.

We sit at a café terrace and watch the Sunday morning activity. There's a lot of cake-buying, the *pasteleria* is doing great trade. Next to it there's a bookshop, so we buy a Spanish–English dictionary for 1200 pesetas. Even our menu Spanish isn't as good as we thought it would be.

For lunch we have *tapas* from the café, then walk around the town eating chocolate ice-creams on a stick. This is pan-American civilisation for you: the ubiquity of industrial ice-cream.

DECISION

So far, we are on el Camino de Santiago. The pilgrim way stretches before us. There are fifteen significant sites before we reach Compostella. Plus however many interesting ones. We can't do them justice. Not in the number of days we have left. We could get to Compostella if we stuck to the motorway and drove fast, straight, blinkered, stopping only to eat and sleep, reading about the places we hadn't seen in the guidebook before going to bed early. We hate travelling like that. Travelling only to arrive and not for the journey. And it would be unbearable in the small hot car.

Sorrowfully we take the decision that has been forming ever since Rocamadour — did we suspect, when we first allowed ourselves to think the thought that we might not go, that we had already decided we wouldn't? That we knew all along but couldn't admit it? Perhaps, but we did have to work up to it … We turn north towards the sea coast and France. Compostela next time.

Sorrowfully ... Not that sorrowfully. It was the great sites of France that we were in love with anyway, that we wanted to visit and revisit. And the small sites, our friends and old haunts. This gives us more time with them. Suddenly we can admit that this is what we really want to do. To stop in one place for a while, a familiar long-friendly place. Not going to Compostela gives us more time in Sévérac, our fondest place in all the world (except for home). We can't resist. Our tongues are already getting ready to speak the dear old familiar French language.

SAN SEBASTIEN

I never imagined that I would spend the greater part of my life so far from the sea as Canberra is, in this high country of dry hot air and winter frost. I grew up by the sea, I love its salt air and its damp breezes. I love seaside towns and the kind of compromises they have to make with their geography, their tenuous hold on the coastline, the way they have to negotiate their survival.

Well, in San Sebastien's case they have done so luxuriously. It's built on a bay, so round and enclosed it's the shape of a cockle-shell, and called Bahia de la Concha, shell bay. On either side the headlands curve in to meet it, and between these is an island, Santa Clara, that protects it further. The inside of the bay is lined with expensive apartments, and there's a palace, the Miramar, built in the nineteenth century by a Hapsburg princess who made the place fashionable.

It's the hour of the afternoon promenade, and there are people walking up and down, up and down, filling the wide pavement of the Playa de la Concha. People move at a measured pace, a kind of dignified amble, and you have to get this right. Try to go too fast and you're ducking and weaving through the crowd, or too slow and people will elbow past. They are good at not getting out of the way; we are the ones who sidestep. Quite proper, we are very amateur promenaders. There are some wonderful babies, in gorgeous perambulators, with lace and frills. A fashion seems to be for a satin coverlet, quilted and embroidered, with a gold name brooch pinned precisely, according to the golden mean. They are on show, these babies. They imply families and friends, other than strangers' eyes looking at them.

The late evening light is beautiful. There's a deep watery haze over the sea and the sinking sun shining through it turns the whole sea silver. The tide is out, and the length of wet sand gleams silver too. People on the beach and boats moored in the bay are misty, ethereal, the whole scene is suffused with this radiance of watery light. None of the promenaders are looking at it, they are engrossed in themselves, the serious business of their conversation, its fierceness.

Later I see a picture of this promenade in a storm. A great wave is rearing up in the air, and raining down over the balustrade; it's six times as high as the people running from it. And the promenade is already some metres above the sand. So even the elegance of San Sebastien is subject to negotiation with a violent sea.

And it hasn't always been so luxurious. As a border stronghold it was often attacked, and seems to have had an uncanny susceptibility to fire — twelve times it burned down. Getting rid of its fortifying walls in 1863 meant that it could expand, and grow into a modern city.

HOTEL

We're staying at the Hotel Europa. We tried the Bahia. Asked to look at the room. Pokey, dingy, ugly, on the main street. Anything quieter? We're taken to a room in the middle of the building. Lace curtains. Behind them the shutters are closed. No they're not. In fact the windows are open as well. They look out on a light well, each side of which is about the width of our window. Thirty centimetres below is a corrugated iron roof. I don't know how high the well goes, I don't want to stick my head out to look. It's the kind of window, when you turn your back on it, it creeps up on you. You turn round to confront it, it sits there with an even more sinister air. It drains the room of light, it's a source of darkness, not illumination. If you slept here it would drain you, too. You could do an Edgar Allan Poe, in this room.

Cosmo has already checked out the Europa. It's more than we can afford. Half as much again as the

Bahia. So we go to the Europa. The room is classy. It's got green apples in a bowl, and a vase of carnations in the bathroom. Which actually works. It's minuscule, as usual. But you don't need extra hands to hold the shower nozzle and beat the shower curtain off while you try to wash yourself. Bathrobes. A minibar, our first. The room really just a pathway round the double bed, but it's handsome, with grand windows. Facing on to the street (same main street as the Bahia) which is full of traffic, and we discover at seven the next morning, being jackhammered. There's a lot of street care going on in Europe, outside our hotel windows, on the roads and motorways we drive down. Philosophically, you'd have to be into a doctrine of becoming; perfection is certainly out, and completion not on the cards. Is this why I am so keen on Romanesque? It is done, it is finished, it's not busy becoming. People knew this when they'd made it, in the tenth century, or the eleventh, and so did their descendants. They built it, and saw that it was good. And let it be. By and large, they are still happy with it.

Not always, of course. Sometimes somebody added extensions in the Gothic manner, or rebuilt bits, or the original building took so long that the style changed, so that the round Romanesque arches of the apse end of a church become pointed Gothic by the front door. But there's plenty of the pure and finished kind. And lots that's impure and finished.

We discover by reading the wrapper on the soap that the Bahia and the Europa belong to the same firm. Maybe the dinginess of the Bahia is a device to drive people into the arms of the Europa. Which belong to polished bright young people, who speak not just French but English too and German. They are good-natured and laugh a lot and make jokes in French and English with Cosmo. One of the jokes which amuses them a lot is deciding that he speaks both languages better than they do. It makes you wish you were rich so that you could always stay in such good-natured places. And this is only three star: there's a five-star offering.

Jackhammers make for early starts. We're looking forward to breakfast; dinner was *tapas* which assuage immediate hunger but don't last long. What's more, we didn't get to bed till 1.30; we walked to the old port and tried a *tapas* bar or two — you feel a bit of an idiot standing in a *tapas* bar and looking up the dishes in a dictionary but it's no more than you deserve and who cares anyway — and wondered about going to a restaurant to eat but didn't feel quite hungry enough and finally sat in a large quiet square called Plaza de la Constitución, whose shape and air were as surreal as a film. It was surrounded by buildings with high arcades, and balconies in rows across each floor. On to these balconies opened hundreds of doors, with numbers over them. Very mysterious, until you discover the square was used as an arena, for bullfights; the numbers are for the spectators' places. There were cafés in and out of the ground floor arcades, and people sitting at them, but the large place was dim and quiet, a good place to sit and think. Perhaps about bullfights, imagining the hot yellow sun providing another kind of surreal angle to the light. Conjuring up benighted memories of sweat and blood and the smells of dust and fear. Ghostly veronicas like dances of death. Maybe it's the knowledge of death that makes this place solemn now. I'm glad we've found it. I think it's important to just sit in places, not do anything, feeling them, getting a sense of them. When you're travelling this is the most important thing of all.

SLEEPLESS IN SPAIN

Spain is difficult for the summer traveller, moving from place to place, but great if you're staying in one spot. Travellers need to get up early for cool morning driving. Then lunch isn't till 2.00 at least, better 2.30. Then it's time for a sleep, a nap, a rest anyway, but you can't do this if you're on the road. Dinner isn't till ten, if you're lucky, more likely eleven. So between late nights and early mornings you risk getting severely underslept.

Next day we decide we'll have lunch before we leave San Sebastien. We've been for a walk along past the Miramar Palace, and watched men playing *pelota* against the high walls on which the promenade is built above the sand. We could stay here for some time, walking about in the daytime, promenading in the evening. There's such pleasure in the sea air, the light.

Stupidly we take the car out of its garage and go to the old port. Nowhere to park, not illegally even.

We drive around like losing players in a board game, constantly thwarted by one-way streets and no-entry signs, till finally we find ourselves on the motorway back to France. No point in planning to eat there; what's too early for lunch in Spain is too late for lunch in France, once you've driven a few kilometres.

So we stop at a restaurant in a lay-by, it will be, after all, an experience, and have some more *tapas*. Industrial, but quite nice at the same time. We eat *raffeones*, squid, knowing that it is the kind that comes ready battered in a cardboard box and usually tastes as though it were reared there too, though it is very tender and the batter quite delicate. Then some *croquetas*, which are potato cakes with a crumbed casing and seasonings. And the *tortilla* isn't too bad. I read in the guidebook that San Sebastien is a gastronomic capital. People eat a lot, and well. Especially in clubs, some thirty of them, for food lovers — men only — who meet and cook up wonderful meals. At the check-out we buy a block of chocolate, strong Spanish chocolate, to console us.

TORTILLA

In Spain this is a kind of omelette, nothing at all to do with the crisp Mexican *tortilla*. It is best made in a frying-pan with a good surface, a non-stick finish of some kind.

One of the most classical is a potato *tortilla*.

Thoroughly cover the bottom of a medium-sized pan with olive oil. Heat.

Dice two large potatoes and fry them in oil until crisp and tender.

Beat together four eggs. Pour over potatoes and cook over moderate heat, stirring and lifting gently until the eggs are set on the bottom and part-way through the egg mixture.

The brave can turn this over, using a plate; cowards like me put it under a hot grill until the surface bubbles and sets. I actually prefer this finish.

It can be eaten warm or cold, and is good picnic food.

There are all sorts of *tortilla* variations. You can add some sliced onion to the potato, or make the omelette with just onions. You can add garlic, and make a version with some courgettes, mushrooms, or peppers. If you are planning to flip the *tortilla* over it must not be made too large, but if you are finishing it under a grill this is not a problem. Herbs can be added for flavouring, and some grated cheese. Cooking it like this it can become a kind of quiche without the pastry shell.

THE CANTABRIC COAST

The roads in and out of San Sebastien are crowded with giant apartment blocks. They have small balconies bravely sporting geraniums, successful ones, and a lot of white washing. White washing is a bit of a mystery flapping around these grubby buildings, in this grimy air. Perhaps these places are the homes of the promenaders of the Playa de la Concha, coming to town to watch the sun set in the sea.

This part of Spain is called the Cantabric coast. Along it and into France is a road called the Corniche Basque with wonderful sea views, a small road and very close to the cliff; you imagine a moment's distraction and you could drive over. Beside it is the massive Atlantic, or really I suppose it's the Bay of Biscay, with great heaving waves. Near Ciboure we stop because Cosmo finds a telephone box and rings up our children and what a surprise they're both home and he has an expensive chat while I take photographs of this most amazing cliff, sheer, anybody could fall off it with the greatest of ease, so I'm surprised I don't feel the panic I felt when walking round the ramparts at Rocamadour where there were perfectly safe fences. Maybe because it's not man-made. This is road, a strip of grass, and great grey spines of rock sheering down to the wild Atlantic.

St-Jean-de-Luz is next; nowhere to park there either so we gaze from the car and go on to Biarritz.

RESORT

We leave the car outside the casino and go into a teashop which is full of ladies eating enormous concoctions of ice-cream and chantilly, great mounds of whipped cream, that they scoop up with little spade-shaped spoons out of silver dishes, and lick with languid tongues into their smug cat faces. We are ascetic: Cosmo has a cup of tea and I have an *orange pressé*. And read the red *Michelin*. There are several cheapish hotels close by.

So we find l'Atalaye, which is on the edge of the plateau of that name, right above the sea and the old port. We take the expensive room: 270 francs, a lot of space. The building is pretty, with round turrets at the corners; our lavatory is in a turret.

Biarritz. I think I have always known the name Biarritz. A resort. Growing up by the sea, I went to other seashores for holidays. A resort didn't mean my kind of seaside town, with immense flat horizons and sand in everything and shabby bungalows and corner shops selling iceblocks and for a small sum filling your billycan with boiling water so you could make tea. HOT WATER, said the signs, in big letters; you can still see the ghosts of them, sometimes, on out-of-the-way faded walls. No. A resort was people dressed like Mrs Simpson and the Prince of Wales, with cafés and golf and gardens sheltered from the salt air and lacy architecture. With paths for nicely shod feet, so that people could look at the sea without getting messed up. How did I as a child know all this? Sometimes I think we spend our early years as detectives, super-sleuths, putting together clues in order to understand the mystery of adult life and the world it inhabits, doing a brilliant job of scouring out every tiny fragment that will help complete the puzzle. Sometimes putting it together a bit lopsided, as though we've looked at it through a window with old warped glass that's a bit bubbled and flawed, or maybe it's the world that's really like that, and we've seen it true. I knew about resorts from years of painstaking fact accumulation, research, and informed speculation.

Bondi has had it in mind to be a resort, at moments. Its hotels have the right wedding-cake image, and there are apartments with bay windows and names like the Ozone and the Biltmore. Its lovely deep curve of beach, seashell-shaped like la Bahia de la Concha at San Sebastien, is just right for promenading, and the street that follows it is called a parade. But it's not elegant, there are joggers, and people with the waterlogged eyes of constant swimmers, nobody puts on elaborate clothes to go and walk beside the beach at Bondi. It's bare feet, and toes in the sand. But of course there are fashions, there's a right way to look, it's sexy, skimpy. This year bare midriffs showing smooth pale brown skin the colour of a crisp biscuit. A bitter almond biscuit. Edible is what the young women look; Mrs Simpson would not have approved. And amid the glamour you've got to be careful of sweaty joggers who'll shove you out of the way, or at least intimidate you, so that they don't lose the rhythm of their run. On the cliff paths their flailing elbows could be fatal. There are plenty of beautiful men and women about, but they don't have the languid strolling glamour of Biarritz. My Biarritz, of the imagination.

THE OLD TOWN

The real one started off as a whaling port. This was in the Middle Ages. During summer a great number of whales would cruise the Bay of Biscay. Lookouts would keep watch from an *atalaye*, which was a kind of watch-tower with a chimney; when they spotted the whales they'd light a fire and send up smoke signals. From ports up and down the coast harpooners would take to the sea in little boats. The catch was divided between the fishermen and the owners of the harpoons. And the priests of Bayonne got their share, the tongue. It was considered a real feast. How did they eat it, I wonder. All gathered round an immense platter, the bishop carving? Or was it cut up into small parcels and sent round the parishes?

The last whale was taken in 1686. It got too difficult, mainly for political reasons: England and Holland chased the French off. Britannia ruling the waves and keeping the whales for herself. The French took to going to Newfoundland for the cod but the British made that too hard also. By the nineteenth century Biarritz was no more than a poverty-stricken village. Then the people of Bayonne got into the habit of going there to bathe. They went on donkeys, or mules, two to a saddle. It was the Empress Eugénie, wife of Napoleon III, who made it fashionable; she knew about it from her Spanish connections.

This is a pattern, all over the world. Working places become pleasure places. Darling Harbour turns from a working port into a glossy commercial

156

development for tourists from home and away. Fun is supposed to be constructed there. Queen's Wharf, in Newcastle, where ships from sail to steam to diesel tied up and did their business, where my father daily caught the boat to the State Dockyard, builds a bar and café and puts out tables for people to sit and watch the traffic of the harbour.

The grimy port can be perceived as beautiful, in a subtle estuarine way. The water turns indigo, the colours of olive oil, pewter grey, the sun sets through the gorgeous man-made clouds of the steelworks. Though it is doubtful whether the café patrons, drinking and talking, notice much of this. But they have chosen this place for its situation, its views, so perhaps they do see it, out of the corners of their eyes.

Le Grill Eugenie

We have dinner at le Grill Eugénie, on a glassed-in terrace in a hotel next door to ours, which doesn't have a restaurant. We're glad of the enclosure, the place outside looks a bit windswept, people walking past are holding their coats to their throats because of the chilly wind, a lovely bracing Atlantic breeze, full of salt and ozone. Not a Mrs Simpson or a Prince of Wales in sight; parkas, tracksuits, Queen-of-England scarves.

I thought le Grill Eugénie might be a bit large and commercial but the food was delicious. I had salmon in the provençale manner, so the menu said; it was raw and marinated. Provence seems an unlikely provenance, salmon not being one of its fish. Not Mediterranean. It was in lovely chunky slices with lots of parsley and green herbs, a tiny bit of finely chopped onion and some good olive oil.

To drink? We're back in the land of Jurançon sec.

Cosmo had grilled tuna, which nowadays is fished off these shores, served with pasta and a *sauce Basquaise* which was definitely of the mild kind. And I ate *pot de feu aux fruits de mer* which I expected to be a runny stew served in a bowl but it came on a plate with a small pile of pasta, and one of those reddish sauces with prawn shells, and in it sitting slices of a whole lot of fish; the waitress told me the names. I understood salmon, *rascasse*, something like *vivier* and there was another whose name I didn't catch. It was all very good fish, with that kind of dense quality that indicates it hasn't been overcooked, it's at that point of perfect tenderness that's still got a faint resistance when you bite into it, which is of course what's meant by *al dente*. That's exactly how you want your fish to be, springy, and it means that it's very fresh. If it's soggy that's a sign that something has gone wrong with it, age, or freezing, and if it's tough and dry and hard it's overcooked. Or else sloppy and falling apart and overcooked. It's easy to ruin fish.

More *fromage de pays*, the local cheese, half cow half sheep, served in thin slices on a plate. Then *île flottante*, which seems to have spread everywhere. I first noticed this dish of custard with islands of meringue floating on top in Paris three years ago. I wondered how they got the meringue so fluffy; did they cheat, perhaps, have some sort of commercial secret, like the incredible high lightness of shop pavlova: how did they get them like that? I suspected some sort of industrial action.

FLOATING ISLAND

This recipe comes from *La Cuisine de Madame Saint-Ange*, which one could perhaps describe as a French Mrs Beeton, except that its being French makes it so entirely different from the English book. Its emphasis is on process; a young woman would acquire it as a bible when she got married, and it would tell her how to do everything she'd ever need. But only cooking; no diagrams on folding napkins or notes on what to do if the butler has an apoplexy. It's a work of genius, if you believe the definition of genius as the infinite capacity for taking pains. No pictures or diagrams, just words.

Madame Saint-Ange begins: '*Ce traditionnel entremets de ménage ...*', thereby referring to one of my favourite topics. This is a dish traditionally made at home. Not the kind of thing that you buy from the *pâtissier*, with complicated assemblage and decoration, nor a dish that in Madame's day you'd have eaten in a restaurant. I think people who cook at home should give some thought to what is suitable under such circumstances, leaving complicated and highly technical work to professionals; certainly not feeling bad because they aren't as clever as somebody whose trade and living it is. It's precisely the homely simple deliciousness of *île flottante* that I love. It's easy enough, but not quick; Madame gives an hour and a quarter, plus cooling time. She calls it *œufs à la neige*, snow eggs, but it is exactly the same as Floating Island. I note that my French dictionary translates *œufs à la neige* as Floating Island, so perhaps what happened is that the English term got turned back into French.

This is such a nice piece of prose that I'm translating pretty much word for word — and for the comfort of beginners.

ŒUFS A LA NEIGE

This traditional household dessert can be slightly difficult for novices only in the matter of the regular shaping of the egg whites, for the poaching or cooking; but you'll get there quickly with our instructions. The poaching is done, as you choose, in boiling water or in the milk which is afterwards used for the cream: it is this last procedure we're using here.

The cream is flavoured to taste with vanilla or lemon ...

The proportion of egg yolks is a little lower than is generally used in *crème anglaise*; but it is necessary to consider that here this cream plays the role of sauce to the dessert. The very small quantity of potato starch [or cornflour] indicated facilitates the execution of the cream ...

Proportions. For 6 people: 6 eggs; 150 grams of caster sugar; 3/4 litre of milk; 175 grams of sugar; a teaspoon of potato starch [or arrowroot or cornflour]; a zest of lemon.

Order of work. The milk. Boil it in a saucepan–frying-pan at least 20 to 22 centimetres in diameter. A saucepan with high sides will make the poaching operation difficult. Add the [caster] sugar, vanilla flavoured, or lemon. [Note: I used only 150 g sugar each time, and no lemon; the sugar was vanilla sugar, that is, I had stored it with a vanilla bean.] Cover, don't let it boil. Watch over the complete melting of the sugar.

The egg whites. First of all spread the sugar on a piece of strong paper, whence it will be easier to let it fall on the stiffly beaten eggs [egg whites: *en neige* is the expression for these].

Whip the whites. [You can turn to page 10 for four closely written pages on how to do this. Briefly: I used a copper bowl and a whisk, as is my wont; it's easy to work out when the right degree of stiffness has been obtained — mainly because you get quite keen to reach this point and stop beating. If using an electric device be very careful not to overbeat. Usual advice applies: no grease near the whites, not a skerrick of yolk in them, everything very clean and dry.] When they are stiff, let fall the sugar in a rain and, carefully, mix it in by cutting and lifting the mass, as directed for the mixing of whites.

To mould and poach the eggs. Put the pan of milk back on the fire. Bring it to boil again. Keep it just simmering.

Take up the egg white with a big spoon [a table-spoon or a serving spoon]. With the blade of an ordinary knife, quickly shape and smooth the white, leaving it rounded so as to give it an egg shape.

Knock the handle of the spoon against the edge of the pan so that the snow egg falls into the boiling milk. [Note that these are called snow eggs both because the whites are whipped into a snow and because the meringues are the shape of eggs.] Repeat the process to make four eggs. No more, because, swelling in the milk, they'll poach badly if they haven't enough room. After a minute and a half, the side dipping in the milk being set, turn the eggs using the handle of a fork. [I have to confess using the soup skimmer I took them out with.] Leave them another 2 minutes. Take them out with a slotted spoon [or soup skimmer]. Drain them by lining up on a cloth...

Continue by fours until all the whites are used. With the quantities given you should get 15 eggs, at least.

Make sure not to leave the eggs too long in the milk, nor to heat the milk too much during the poaching of the eggs. If they are cooked too much, they collapse, lose their shape, are no longer even edible. Their cooking consists in just firming only the part dipped at first in the milk, nothing more than what is necessary to turn them over straightaway. That's why it's important to turn the eggs over by beginning with the one put first in the pan.

Madame Saint-Ange goes on to tell you that the white will slip easily off the spoon if you dip it in water first, and that you can also mould it using two spoons.

Now you have to make the cream. You could turn to page 911 for several pages of instructions, but I'm going to abbreviate.

You beat the egg yolks with the starch (this is a tip, it saves the eggs turning, as they have a nasty habit of doing suddenly, 'decomposing', going granular like scrambled eggs) until thick and creamy (forming a ribbon). Strain the still hot poaching milk, and add it little by little to the yolks, continuing to beat. Put in a saucepan and heat gently, still stirring with a wooden spoon, until ready to set.

The setting point is reached when the light froth which covers the surface of the cream dissipates. At this moment, when you remove the spoon you will see its back covered with the cream like a light varnish — without thickness … It's necessary to take the pan off the fire straightaway. [I would add, to get it out of the saucepan as quickly as possible, especially if it's thick and heat retentive.]

Strain again into a shallow terrine. Put a spoon in it, and every three or four minutes, as it cools, stir it, in order to prevent a skin forming — otherwise you'll have to heat it and strain it again, says Madame. Hmm.

I sat beside it and read a book, every few pages giving it a stir. I couldn't bear to do all that over again.

When it's quite cold arrange the eggs, the islands, over its surface. I have to say that my islands were floating in a very crowded sea, it was more of a log jam. Except of course for the marvellous lightness of the meringue — and there's the answer to my question, it's not industrial lightness, it's classical. I used 70 g free-range eggs and got exactly fifteen snow eggs; when I was forming them they seemed about the size of generous hen's eggs but swelled greatly. I couldn't fit them all on my sea, or pond. But that wasn't a problem, especially remembering the comment that the custard is a sauce, I just served people extra islands. Next time I'll put the same amount of custard into two shallow dishes.

This recipe seems to me an image of the pure magic of cooking. So few ingredients: eggs, sugar, milk, vanilla; and so plain, the dish made from them so marvellously a new creation. Not difficult, as Madame says; it seems to take longer to read than to make. It's certainly taken me longer to write out.

For my own amusement I checked what Mrs Beeton said. Her Floating Island is a pudding of whipped cream topped with rocky blobs of whipped egg whites mixed with jam. But she has a recipe for Snow Eggs. See what I mean about the French book and process.

MRS BEETON'S SNOW EGGS

Ingredients. — 3 eggs, 1 pint of milk, sugar, essence of vanilla.

Method.— Boil up the milk, sweeten to taste, and flavour with vanilla. Whisk the whites of eggs to a stiff froth, put 1 tablespoonful at a time into the boiling milk, and poach until firm. Turn two or three times during the process, and as each portion is cooked, drain and place in a glass dish. Beat the yolks of the eggs, add them to the milk, and strain into the jug. Stand the jug in a saucepan of boiling water, and stir the contents until they thicken. Let the custard cool, stirring occasionally meanwhile, then pour over and round the snow eggs, and serve.

Time. — About 1¼ hours. Sufficient for 6 or 7 persons.

It's almost laconic in comparison, but it's all there, provided you know how to read it. This strikes me as a useful recipe for Cook: when the mistress asks her to make Snow Eggs for dinner, she looks them up and turns out a marvellous dish because she knows how; Madame Saint-Ange you could follow if you'd never boiled water before. In fact she was concerned that young women were being educated in all sorts of studies like law, medicine, philosophy, painting, astronomy, and music, that they learned everything but cooking, so in 1893 she started a journal to teach them, and eventually did a book.

Notice that Mrs Beeton uses half the number of eggs for the same number of people.

Footnote: Reading Brillat-Savarin I have discovered that he organises people and food into three categories, what you could describe as rich, prosperous, modest. *Ile flottante* is in the bottom level.

THE SEA

After we've eaten the sweet eggy pudding, dreamily we eat it, that's what it seems to need, we walk across the square and look over the edge. It's built quite high above the sea. Below is the old port, with the tide coming in. We walk down some zigzag steps to this, *le port des pêcheurs*: it's actually three rooms. The rocks that were originally here have been joined up with stone walls. There's an entrance round one side, through a channel between one of the rooms and a small cliff-edged promontory, where the waves are crashing and swirling in the narrow space. Ships must negotiate this channel into one after the other of the three rooms, and be safe from the storms of the Atlantic. You could imagine fierce storms on this coast, its edges so fretted and rocky. I remember sailing across the Bay of Biscay in an ocean liner, feeling seasick to death and having to pack for a dawn arrival in Tilbury in the morning, and with a small baby to care for. That was the only time I've ever minded babies' nappies. Even on this fine summer night, with the earlier breeze stilled, the sea is not calm. You'd think it would be easy to be dashed against the sides of the channel, your boat wrecked a few metres from safety. I'm thinking, if the port's as dangerous as this, how much worse is the sea?

There are little houses crowded up against the cliff, on the wharf in front of the port. They look as though people live in them, with their piles of wood for burning. And a couple of cafés with brilliant lights strung between poles; one is la Casa de Juan, and serves *tapas*. This is interesting because it had seemed to us that there was really no leakage across the border. I'd expected some sort of osmotic mingling between France and Spain. You hear so much about Europe, and people worrying about the flattening out of local cultures, their mushing down into a general featureless characterless community, but the ancient separateness of customs and eating habits is hardly eroded. Even the fact that up and down here is the Basque country doesn't prevent its being still French or Spanish.

It's a strange area this wharf, a bit wild, with tattooed seamen, well, tattooed men anyway, and people with motorbikes; it's as though the rough old fishing village has remained beside the watering place of the bourgeois empress. You can imagine Joseph Conrad describing its *louche* ways and fishy smells, its tough women and unnatural light; pass the bottle, he would say, and tell you a story of seafaring passions. When we leave to walk up a zigzag path to the plateau at the top we're climbing from the dangerous trade of the old fishing port, under the graceful tamarisk trees of nineteenth-century promenades, to the prosperous holiday town. To our hotel which is a bit of a folly, with its red-roofed pepper-pot turrets.

I'm not sure how fashionable Biarritz is now. The people we see aren't young, apart from those down at the old port. Up here they're distinctly middle-aged, not to mention dowdy. Though in the shopping streets there are plenty of surf shops. *Ecoles de surf*, they're called, surf schools, though they don't look as though they give lessons. And next day, lying in the still, concentrated sunshine of the sheltered bathing beach are dozens of bare-breasted women. All those nipples pointing to the sky make my Australian sensibilities uneasy. Sunburnt nipples. Don't they know about skin cancers? Are they placing an unhealthy level of trust in the solidity of their ozone layer? People don't wear hats either.

I like Biarritz. I like its mighty Atlantic breakers, which remind me of the violent Pacific at Merewether, where I grew up. I like its walks up and down cliffs and along the plateaux of its seashores. I like its massive rocks, that you can walk out on to. One you reach by a long metal bridge, and on top of it is a large white statue of the Virgin Mary. There's a legend of some fishermen caught in a storm; as they struggle against the sea they make a vow that they'll raise a statue of the Virgin on a rock if they get back to port. Well, they do, and they do, and now tourists can walk safely out to le Rocher de la Vierge, buy postcards and souvenirs from its small kiosk, observe the banks of floodlights underpinning the statue, and stare at the heaving waters swelling and shredding themselves against the rock, though this is the sunniest of summer days.

You have to respect the sea around Biarritz. This for me would be its charm; holidays by a sea that might at any moment erupt into violence. Like Sunday walking parties round the crater of a volcano.

On one of the clifftops there's a war memorial, a large bronze of people grieving. It's moving because it's not military, it's ordinary people full of pain, suffering the effects not proclaiming the splendour of war. It must be quite new. France is full of war memorials, mainly from the first war, the second being difficult to commemorate without ambiguity. Often just pillars with lists of names. I stop and read them, these names so weighty with untimely death, trying to imagine the young men and the lives they didn't have. Names are poignant. They are emblems of fragility, and yet they remain long after the people they belonged to. The War Memorial in Canberra has great bronze panels of names; it's important to read them. I think of parents naming their children with such hope, as always we do, to have them end up on a list of casualties. Look at that word, casualty: you'd think it meant somebody not paying attention, being careless, and you can certainly believe that of many military commanders. But what it is connected with is chance: causality, accidentalness, luck of the bad kind.

I'm not the only one to think of the Prince of Wales in Biarritz. Among the usual streets, Jean Jaures and Carnot and the Republic, the Bellevue and the Imperatrice, there's a boulevard named after him: boulevard du Prince de Galles. Though which one? There's also an Avenue Edouard VII, and another de la Reine Victoria. As well as a rue Pringle. I wonder who Pringle was? The twin-set man?

BAYONNE

The double-saddled donkey track from Bayonne to Biarritz has disappeared under suburbs. You can't any longer tell where one starts and the other stops. But once you get to the centre of Bayonne you are in the presence of ancient events. A lot of history. For a child of the new world, the volume of this is a spectacle in itself.

The city was already important in the first century BC, since its conquerors built a wall round it. It was attractive because it was a port, on a river with a wide safe estuary; well, safe compared to the rocky sea coast at Biarritz. A lot of people coveted it: Visigoths, Gascons, Arabs, Normans.

At one time it was part of the duchy of Aquitaine. One of its better known dukes was Huon, who accidentally killed a son of Charlemagne. He was offered a pardon if he would go to Babylon, cut the emir's beard and pull out four of his teeth, bringing these trophies back to the emperor. A pardon that was no pardon, being impossible, you'd think. But with the help of a charming dwarf it was done. The dwarf was called Oberon; Shakespeare took him up some centuries later, and stretched him in a number of ways, into the tall and handsome king of the fairies. Huon seems to have married the emir's daughter, Esclarmonde.

This tale is also according to a *Chanson de Geste*, a thirteenth-century reconstruction of the eighth-century story. Like Roland's, the amazing adventures of the duke owe something to the embroidery of time.

The last duke of Aquitaine was succeeded by a daughter Eleanor, who was married to the king of France, Louis VII, in 1137. He was an ascetic and religious man, who lived like a monk; Eleanor was frivolous. She took a brilliant court with her when she accompanied him on the second crusade, and caused a scandal at Antioch, so when they got back to France Louis divorced her. She married Henry Plantagenet, who at that time was count of Anjou; when he became king of England two years later their combined lands were bigger than the French king's, which led to three centuries of struggle between the two countries. This is the Henry who murdered his archbishop Thomas à Becket; when he was an old man, his sons, among whom were Prince John and Richard I, Richard the Lionheart, of Robin Hood fame, urged on by their mother Eleanor, rebelled against him.

During one of the ongoing battles, at the time of Joan of Arc, when the French were besieging Bayonne which was at the time in the hands of the English, there was a miracle: a great white cross appeared in the sky, surmounted by a crown which turned into a *fleur de lys*. The people of Bayonne threw down their red-cross banners and became French. They regretted it. They lost the English market (the Plantagenets loved claret, which was grown in Bordeaux and shipped to England) that made their port's fortune, the French interfered with their liberties far more than the distant English and would no longer let them conduct their affairs in Gascon. They realised that the miracle had tricked them.

All this in the name Bayonne. And volumes still to come.

Several more claims to fame. One is the arms factories that gave the world a steel blade on the end of a gun, the bayonet. Another is the *jambon de Bayonne*, the raw ham, a prosciutto style, which is very fine. The third is chocolate.

CHOCOPHILIA

Chocolate is a mind-bending substance so people get addicted to it. Madame de Sévigné said, 'It pleases you for a while, then suddenly it inflames you with a fever that leads you to death.' So when Robert Dessaix asked me to review a book about chocolate for 'Books and Writing' I was keen. Chocolate is occasionally a theme of our conversation: Robert is addicted, I am not. But I am very fond of wine. I should probably say addicted here too. So we offer one another these habits, hobbies, passions, these incipient vices, not quite understanding the other's taste but accepting it. And of course recognising that we could give them up whenever we wanted to; it's not the effect we care about, it's the flavour. But we have no plans for doing so — giving them up, oh no.

It was the end of the year, the programme was to go to air on New Year's Day, so it could afford a frivolous moment. Well, seven minutes, quite enough for a small book. It's called *A Passion for Chocolate* by Pamela Allardice, and subtitled 'How to turn your love affair with chocolate into a lasting relationship'. It looks rather like a CD in size and shape, with a cover half of swirled brown and white chocolate, half a wash of purple and pink. The whole effect rather bilious I think. The contents are divided too; half history, half recipes. Most of the recipes are too rich, so rich that just reading them is troubling. Too much cream, too much butter, too much unctuous cocoa product.

But the history is fine. You know bits of it, but it's good to have it all together. Chocolate was the drink of the Aztecs and the Incas — a drink, notice; the chocolate tablet is a nineteenth-century invention, an industrial creation. It was a drink for warriors, cowards weren't allowed any. You can see why, when you read the recipe for making it: chillies, pepper, aniseed, and of course no sugar. The emperor Montezuma drank a lot of it, maybe thirty cups a day, out of golden goblets, and particularly before visiting his wives. As well as being an aphrodisiac, it was fortifying. Cortéz noted that men could go a whole day without food if they'd drunk a cup of chocolate.

Montezuma gave Cortéz the recipe for his xocotlatl because he thought his visitor was a god, an incarnation of Quetxalcoatl the Plumed Serpent, who gave the gift of the cacao tree in the first place. Cortéz took the recipe, and in return murdered Montezuma and plundered the rest of his treasures.

Cocoa beans were a unit of currency for the Aztecs. Four would buy a pumpkin, a 'tolerably good' slave could cost a hundred, a prostitute be had for ten. When Cortéz took them back to the king of Spain they remained for a long time the food of the rich. The Spanish tried to keep them a secret from the rest of the world and for a while succeeded. Dutch and English pirates who captured cargoes of them threw the beans overboard, calling them sheep shit.

Bayonne became a centre of chocolate when the Jews were chased out of Spain and Portugal, after the Christians had got rid of the Moors. They brought their trade of roasting and grinding with them, and the locals quickly picked it up.

The beans were dried and crushed into a powder, sometimes formed into little cakes, then mixed with water. The Spaniards had the idea of using milk and cream and sweetening it with sugar. The important thing was to whisk it — for perhaps an hour — so that the chocolate frothed. When Anne of Austria married Louis XIII (a baby at the time) she brought with her to France a maid whose only job was to make the queen's chocolate. Invitations to drink it with her were important events at court.

A whole paraphernalia of chocolate drinking implements came with the ceremony. Tea drinking has its teapots and cups and caddies and spirit kettles. Chocolate had carved and gilded boxes to keep the cakes in, and platters with matching cups and spoons, and swizzle sticks to whip up fresh froth, and later china pots with right-angled, right-handed straight handles.

As with all aristocratic delicacies, there were those who conspired to bring chocolate to the people. The Spanish monopoly was broken, and the capture of Jamaica provided flourishing plantations. By the end of the seventeenth century there were chocolate houses all over Europe, centres for social and intellectual life. London had Swifts, and White's, and the Cocoa Tree (a hangout of Tories). White's was in St James Street; the first issue of the *Tatler* announced that from it would emanate accounts of gallantry, pleasure, and entertainment. Connection between more serious newspapers and chocolate houses followed.

Samuel Pepys was an early patron; he got into the habit of taking chocolate in the mornings — *jucalette* he called it. He said it was delicious but expensive. And good for hangovers. After celebrating the coronation of Charles II in 1661 he wrote in his diary that he:

> ... waked in the morning with my head in a sad taking through last night's drink, which I am very sorry for. So rose and went with Mr Creed to drink our morning draught, which he did give me in chocolate to settle my stomach.

This is not a hangover cure I have seen recommended elsewhere.

By the early eighteenth century, all of Europe was taking chocolate. Sometimes with claret and egg yolks to strengthen it. Sometimes made up into a kind of custard with arrowroot and milk. I'm fascinated by the glamour of this chocolate taking, I'd like to know more about it.

Of course, there's been the book and the movie that take their name from the habit: *Like Water for Chocolate* — sometimes the movie was called *Like Water for Hot Chocolate*, so that people would not confuse it with the hard tablet kind.

So in Pamela Allardice's book I turned to what she calls The Ultimate Hot Chocolate. I was bitterly disappointed. Perhaps I should say sickeningly sweetly disappointed. You dissolve three marsh-mallows in hot milk, add cocoa and drinking chocolate and cognac, pour into a mug, decorate with three more marshmallows, dust with more cocoa and drink while hot. I can make no comment on this recipe since I didn't try it. Except to say that it's a pity Allardice didn't have a go at recreating the original drink for warriors. Apart from the cognac hers is what small children have in cafés when their parents are taking coffee, which has supplanted chocolate as the adult drink. Though I wouldn't wish the marshmallows on children either.

For something more like the real thing you could try the recipe in *Larousse Gastronomique*:

Preparation of Chocolate (Beverage)

Chocolat — a generous ounce (40 grams) of good sweet chocolate is needed for a breakfast cup. Put the chocolate broken up into pieces with a small quantity of water or hot milk in a casserole on a gentle heat. Cover the pan, let the chocolate soften, remove from the fire and whip into a smooth paste with a whip or wooden spoon; add first of all two or three tablespoons of boiling liquid (water or milk) to dilute the paste, then the rest of the liquid, still boiling, continuing to stir all the time. To retain the full aroma of the chocolate (the same applies to cocoa) it must never be allowed to boil.

Larousse quotes Brillat-Savarin divulging the secret of the Mother Superior of the Convent of the Visitation at Belley:

'When you want to taste good chocolate,' said that religious gourmande, 'make it the night before, in a faience coffee pot, and leave it. The chocolate becomes concentrated during the night and this gives it a much better consistency.'

I enjoyed the history in Allardice's book. It's more exciting than the recipes, however seriously detailed they may be. Their sugariness sets my teeth on edge and the utter excess of their chocolatiness makes me feel a bit queasy. Imagine a chocolate cake in layers sandwiched with white chocolate cream and milk chocolate cream and decorated with chocolate curls.

It's daunting. But then I'm not a chocoholic. Maybe aficionados are filled with ecstasy at the mere thought. But I'm not sure that chocophiliacs would like them any better; Robert's favourite is chocolate as plain and bitter as possible.

The mere thought is itself an interesting idea. The mere thought of these is enough for me. I am happy to be a vicarious chocolate eater. Reading about it is sufficient, in fact dwelling on these recipes could put me off eating altogether. I feel stuffed with the words. I offer this as a hint for dieting.

I did try one of the recipes, being a conscientious book reviewer, and anyway it intrigued me. It's a cake called Featherlight Gateau: 'a gorgeous name for a sinfully gorgeous gateau'.

Featherlight Gateau

 125 grams unsalted butter
50 grams dark cooking chocolate, chopped
6 x 60 gram eggs, separated
1/3 cup (75 g) caster sugar
1 1/2 tablespoons plain flour
24 chocolate squares, or 24 after dinner mints
cocoa for dusting

1. Preheat the oven to 180°C.
2. Grease and lightly flour a 24 cm round spring form cake pan.
3. Melt the butter and chopped chocolate in the top of a double boiler, stirring to combine.

4. Beat the egg yolks and sugar until thick and pale. Fold the melted chocolate mixture into the egg yolk mixture and mix until well combined. Gently fold in the flour.

5. Beat the egg whites until stiff peaks form and then gently fold through the egg yolk mixture.

6. Pour three-quarters of the mixture into the prepared pan and bake for 40 minutes.

7. When baked the cake should have shrunk slightly from the sides of the pan. Allow it to cool in the pan and it should sink in the middle as it cools.

8. When completely cool, remove the sides of the pan from the cake and pour the reserved quarter of the mixture into the hollow on top of the cake. Take a little of the mixture and spread it thickly around the sides of the cake, spreading the remainder evenly over the top.

9. Place the cake on to a plate or serving dish and then begin arranging the chocolate squares around the sides, making sure that each one overlaps the others. Cut remaining squares into triangles with a hot knife and then press these triangles into the top of the cake.

10. Refrigerate cake for 1 hour, then remove and dust with cocoa powder before cutting with a hot knife to serve.

Serves 12.

You can see why the idea of it fascinated me. Its post-modernity. Its denial of the significant dichotomy established by Levi Strauss in the title of his book, *The Raw and the Cooked*. There are circumstances for eating raw cake; children are allowed to scrape out mixing bowls. Though sometimes they don't want to, which is difficult for would-be indulgent mother and grandmother cooks. It's an image from a 1950s-style happy advertising family: pretty aproned tiny-waisted wife baking, Brylcreem husband licking the beaters, or beaming upon the children doing so. Loving and playful, the beating absolutely confined to the neat little electrical machine that has assumed the drudgery. But it's not the serious part of the eating. That comes when proud wife whips the cake out of the oven, lofty, puffed up, a transformation into a creation quite other. She's clever and good to be able to do this.

Whereas there is something quite disturbing about a cake which gives equal value to the raw and the cooked. That says both these states are equally delicious. We accept this in some circumstances, fruits for instance; apples may be stewed, peaches may be poached, and certain vegetables like carrots or cauliflower can be eaten either way, but not usually cakes, and not usually anything in both states simultaneously. That's what intrigued me about this recipe. I could eat my cake, or should I say *gâteau*, and keep its subversion. And notice what the recipe says: it should sink in the middle as it cools.

How wonderful. Who has never looked with despair at a cake, come out of the oven puffed up and lofty, as it sank in the middle, and felt the stomach-hollow weight of failure sinking with it? Not with the Featherlight Gâteau. It's supposed to behave like that. And it did, beautifully. I felt some qualms, but reminded myself that this was how it was meant to be. The raw part spread nicely, was shiny and sticky.

I have a confession to make, though. I couldn't quite come at the studding with squares of chocolate, nor the dusting with cocoa. Lily-gilding seemed innocuous compared with the chocolate coating of chocolate decoration on the chocolate icing on chocolate cake. I didn't think it needed it, it was delicious as it was. Though better the first day than the second. By then it was very slightly rubbery. Again I beat the egg whites in the copper bowl. Which I do like doing. I suppose because it works so well, you sit with the bowl in your lap and the transformation of slimy egg whites into a quite new substance, an opaque stiff foam that holds its peaks on the beater, is satisfying. It's possible that it won't happen, that there'll be a morsel of yolk in the whites, or the bowl or the beater is a bit greasy, or something imponderable has prevented it, so when you get it right it's an achievement, you can enjoy it. I don't do many things that involve a direct outcome on a physical object these days, it's all words on paper and ideas in heads, and arguments and theories and policies. For the same reason I like gardening, but that's not so immediate as egg whites.

The theory is that whipped egg whites are bulkier and lighter when done by hand in a copper bowl with a balloon whisk. The machine is more violent so the speed and violence mean less air is incorporated and the result is one kind of commercial product, easier but not so good.

There's also a close relationship between the beater and the beaten. Sometimes you may be tired and hand the bowl over to someone else to have a go, but this is dangerous, it almost never works, as though the eggs can tell the difference, and sulk, refuse to perform. This sounds silly, but I would never change beaters in mid-beat. The same with mayonnaise.

Anyway, when I folded the whites into the chocolate mixture I did it quickly and delicately and not very thoroughly which is good for a souffle where little pockets of egg white make it very fluffy, but in the chocolate cake with its longer cooking they were a bit dry. However, the eaters of the cake had no problems with this kind of quibble, which is typical cook's anxiety and comes from examining too closely the finished product.

COCOA TREES

The biological name of the cocoa tree is *Theobroma cacao*, *Theobroma* meaning food of the gods, recalling that long-ago gift of the Plumed Serpent, whom Montezuma supposed to be incarnated in Cortéz. Xochiquetzal, goddess of love and happiness, provided its blossoms.

Cocoa beans have always needed to be carefully processed in order to turn them into chocolate. The beans grow inside fat pods and are scraped out along with some of the pulp; they ferment which develops the flavour. Then they're dried in the sun, roasted, and broken into small nibs, the shell winnowed away. The final quality of the chocolate depends on the skill in the grinding and refining of the nibs, to produce a rich dark liquor which turns solid. An educated palate can distinguish the different flavours of cocoa beans from Jamaica, Martinique, Guadaloupe, Brazil, Guyana, Ecuador. The best is said to come from Venezuela and Guatemala.

It's rich in fat; a Dutchman called Van Houten developed a way of getting rid of this, by treating it with an alkali which darkened it and destroyed part of the flavour, but saponified the fats. This is cocoa, a good restorative drink but not so delicious as real chocolate — and I don't mean what's called drinking chocolate, which is cocoa and sugar, designed to dissolve easily. Cocoa was drunk — maybe still is — by sailors, with rum whenever possible.

When I was a student I went to Melbourne University to do some research and stayed at St Mary's, a Catholic women's college. It was vacation, and the inmates still in residence invited me to supper, and made cocoa in some dangerous way, on an electric fire, I think, because they weren't allowed to cook in their rooms. This was the nearest I ever got to a dormitory feast; the girls were university students but sitting with them in dressing-gowns and slippers in the excitement of this clandestine activity felt like being at a boarding school. At least as it was in the books I read. Of course you shouldn't drink cocoa going to bed; it's far too stimulating.

Brand names

These days, when somebody says chocolate, most of us think of the hardened form, the tablets which can be snapped and nibbled. Or in the plural they come in boxes, filled with creams soft or hard or runny liqueur, or nuts or ginger or plums. All these are early nineteenth-century inventions, and it's interesting that the names of the people who developed the processes are still today's brand names: Cadbury, Fry, Lindt, Rowntree, Van Houten, Suchard, Nestlé. Though goodness knows who actually owns the companies by now.

There are also some tricky practices. For instance chocolate may be entirely defatted of its own natural cocoa butter and then reconstituted with inferior fat. You need to read labels carefully. Mention of palm oil is very suspicious. Soy products are a dead give-away. Hydrolising and hydrogenation add sinister meaning. Expensive chocolates may behave purely, though there are no guarantees, except cost, and then it's only that it's quite certain that cheap chocolate will be inferior, not that expensive will be good.

I like chocolate that is strong and bitter with hardly any sugar. And no milk. Club chocolate, for instance. It's worth noticing the label of this: a gentleman in an armchair, reading a paper, a small coffee cup by his side. The lines of this drawing are Art Deco; it's as though bitter chocolate has such a sure market that there's no need to keep changing the advertising. Of course this in itself might be a clever commercial gimmick.

SAVOURY CHOCOLATE

Chocolate doesn't have to be a sweetmeat. It can be used in savoury dishes to thicken and enrich. It's not uncommon in Mexican cookery, and Spanish, and in Italy you can I believe buy chocolate pasta.

SAUCE AU VIN DE MEDOC

This isn't a sauce, but a stew; the word means stew in the Bordelais area, which of course is quite close to Bayonne, and is probably where the chocolate in this dish comes from. This recipe is based on Elizabeth David's.

Take a rabbit jointed, a kilo of stewing beef and a kilo of pork, chopped in large chunks, brown them in olive oil. Add 4 cloves of garlic chopped, 3 onions, 3 carrots, cover with a bottle of red wine. Add bay leaf, parsley, and thyme, a teaspoon of sugar and a square of chocolate. Add extra water to cover the meat, and simmer for 4 to 5 hours. There'll be a lot of juice; this is a dish for serving with plenty of bread, and the left-over sauce can be served with eggs, either poured over them in egg dishes or with the eggs poached in it.

TO DRINK

What to drink with chocolate is always a problem. Not with these savoury dishes, but with sweet ones.

Simca, Simone Beck, who wrote *Mastering the Art of French Cookery* with Julia Child and Louise Bertholle reckons you should drink red wine — she recommends a fine old Bordeaux from Margaux. Maybe this is the Bayonne connection again. 'In my house I would continue pouring red wine,' she says, and it does work very well, especially where the chocolate is bitterish, not too creamy and squishy. Of course I am speaking as one who given a choice between red wine and chocolate would choose the red wine every time. Real chocophiles probably don't care about the drink at all.

It shouldn't be thought that people who claim to be addicted to chocolate are making excuses for simple greed. Apparently it does work on the brain. It contains phenylethylamine, a natural amino acid which is said to elevate moods — to give you a high. This may be an explanation of chocolate's energy-giving properties. One brand actually calls itself Energy Chocolate. But it's also full of useful things like calcium, phosphorus, potassium, thiamine, riboflavin, niacin, vitamin A. And magnesium, which is good for PMT sufferers. And of course there's carbohydrates and fat.

Brillat-Savarin had a high opinion of it.

Persons who drink chocolate regularly are conspicuous for unfailing health and immunity from the host of minor ailments which mar the enjoyment of life; they are also less inclined to lose weight ...

What a pity that's no longer a good thing.

He recommends it flavoured with amber, from ambergris.

DEATH BY CHOCOLATE

There seems to be something about chocolate that leads its aficionados to excess. Elizabeth David can speak with the fine austerity which was part of her character as a food writer of that traditional picnic food, a piece of chocolate and a Marie biscuit, but chocophiles don't believe that less is more. I thought that Allardice's Triple Chocolate Surprise, mentioned earlier, went about as far as the cocoa bean could go, but I came across a book called *Death by Chocolate* and discovered I was wrong. I'd noticed dessert restaurants of that name; here was the dessert that claimed to have started it all. It's got six elements: cocoa meringue, chocolate mousse, a chocolate brownie layer (made of Simply the Best Brownie Batter), chocolate ganache, mocha mousse, and mocha rum sauce.

You assemble all these layers in a spring-form tin, starting with brownie, then ganache (a mixture of cream, butter, and the ch. word), meringue, mocha mousse, more brownie, more ganache. Finally pipe stars of the chocolate mousse all over the top. Serve on a pool of the mocha rum sauce.

Each slice of this, says its author Marcel Desaulniers of The Trellis restaurant in Virginia, has 1354 calories, or 5687 kilojoules. Choc horror. A woman would have to chop wood for three-and-a half hours to use up that many kilojoules, or walk for thirteen-and-a-half hours. Desaulniers does say his restaurant serves quite large helpings.

The recipe for Death by Chocolate is the last in the book. There are others, with names like Mocha Madness, Ch. Phantasmagoria, Ch. Transportation, Ch. Devastation, Ch. Demise, Caramel Rum Delirium Ice Cream Cake, all under the chapter heading Ch. Dementia. (Of course he writes the word in full.) Such names make you wonder whether the addiction to chocolate is for its mind-altering qualities, or because the mind is already altered.

REST AREA

After Bayonne we get on to the motorway and now we are retracing our path for a bit; this is the road that brought us from Pau to Salies-de-Béarn. Motorways in France as elsewhere have occasional stopping places, where you can pull off, for food or petrol. They are usually midget Los Angeles in their complications of flyovers and clover leaves, and you can never go back the way you came. Some are more than comfort stops, they have what they describe as a cultural vocation. These are *les aires à thème*. *Aire* means literally area, as in the Australian rest area; the English term is lay-by. The motorway company sees itself as having a duty to 'inscribe the *autoroute* in the bosom of a cultural and historic heritage'. This is a good example of French being able to be more flowery and noble than English would ever dare.

So the Aire des Pyrénées has for its theme the countryside, with a panorama of the *pic du Midi* and an orientation table. The Aire de Caissargues is archaeological, it's got the columns of the ancient theatre of Nîmes reconstituted on its site. The Aire de Port is surrounded by water and has an exhibition on the making of the *canal du Midi*, whose marvellous ruled banks and still water make you wish you were sailing down it on a barge, not driving down an *autoroute*. What's great about canals is that they were built for commercial, industrial, business purposes yet they are so calm.

We stop at l'Aire d'Hastingues, which celebrates the pilgrimage to Compostela. It's built as near as possible to the crossing of three of the four great routes. '*Autoroutes du Sud de la France* have chosen to place the *aire* under the sign of the pilgrimage and to take account of the particularity of the place: the meeting of the motorway with these millenary ways.' There's a large exhibition hall built in the shape of a scallop-shell, with seven footpaths radiating into it to symbolise the seven routes beginning in France. On one of these paths is an enormous statue of a pilgrim, in bronze, dressed in cape and cockle-shell hat, with his staff and scrip, not Romanesque, more Rodinesque, but rather magnificent. Inside the building you can follow the stages a pilgrim would make; instead of the stations of the cross, the stages of the pilgrimage.

It's a curious place, a paradoxical place, that knows its own contradictions: on an *autoroute* of speeding cars and hurtling lorries a stopping place that celebrates ancient footpaths. The building itself is glossy, a bit slick, but it's keen to be a work of art housing works of art, even if it's self-conscious about them. It has assembled an impressive list of experts to set it up. There's something touching in its seriousness. Here's a useful bit from one of its pamphlets:

> The success of the pilgrimage and the material organisation along its routes developed little by little cultural exchanges, but also commerce between Spain and its neighbouring countries. These quite diverse aspects — dimensions religious, political, artistic, and economic — make of the pilgrimage to St James of Compostela and its ways one of the major phenomena characterising occidental culture.

Rather stickjaw prose, but interesting sentiments.

The conjunction of the roadside flag of Europe, with its ring of yellow stars on a blue field, and the cockle-shell of the pilgrimage, is a reminder that the new Europe ought to be thought of as a recreation of the old Europe of Christendom, that getting together over things that matter is not a twentieth-century invention. Witness the miraculous works of art that line the route. The legend itself might be improbable, a beat-up, a fraud, a construction long after the event, and Francis Drake right when he dismissed Santiago de Compostela as a stronghold of pernicious superstition, yet it has called forth some of the brightest moments of our civilisation. This lay-by is a good place to remind yourself of them.

And its name? L'Aire d'Hastingues? It's a memory of those days when Aquitaine was part of England, and refers to a nearby walled town, a *bastide*, which Edward I ordered his seneschal, John Hastings, to establish in 1289. A fortified gate remains, with some fifteenth- and sixteenth-century houses, and there's a footpath leading to it from the rest area.

COUNTRY INN

So far we've been staying in towns or villages where parking is always difficult, because of either their antiquity or their modern busyness. So we decide to try the middle of the countryside. We stop at a place outside Pontacq, a big country hotel, a kind of inn, called the Béarn Bigorre, built probably in the fifties, set in fields with rows of trees round it and gravelled paths, well back from a not very busy road. We get a choice of several identical large rooms which seem identically comfortable but later when we try the bed we realise we shouldn't have chosen the room according to our preference in the colour of wallpaper (I thought the pink daisies went better with the pink bedspread than orange roses did) but according to the comfort of the beds. This one sloped steeply to the middle, so we spent the night in somnambulistic cliff-hanging.

It's one of those places that has different wall-paper in every room: big entrance hall, enormous dining-room, lounge room, breakfast room-cum-bar — it's taken advantage of being in the middle of fields to build itself generous spaces — and every room has a completely different pattern of colourful wallpaper. The decorators were people of catholic tastes where wallpaper was concerned, so long as it was gaudy, and indulged them all. Lots of plastic flowers to clash, including a large orange tree in a tub on the stair landing. For a moment I thought it was real, and was charmed. The fantasy, the ambi-tion, of an orange tree on a staircase. When I got close enough (quite close it had to be) to see it was plastic I lost all this admiration, except perhaps a grudging respect for its skill as a fake. Which was momentary; it immediately looked tawdry, even from a distance. Evidently what I had been admir-ing was also the difficulty of keeping an orange tree alive in an awkward place. And of course this is authenticity again, not wanting a representation, an imitation, but the real thing. Why shouldn't the plastic version appear as an icon, to remind, to pic-ture forth the beauties of small radiant fruit on dark green branches? It just doesn't. You can't talk your-self into it.

An icon doesn't imitate, it represents the real; it imagines it in another medium. Christ in a mosaic, Mary as a small wooden statue with a man-child on her knee: not from any distance could you mistake

them for the flesh. That's not what they mean. So
when something like the orange tree does trick you
for a moment into thinking it is real, you feel
cheated, and so irritated, perhaps a bit angry.

It's not too late in the day, for a change we have
time, nothing special to do, we can sit on the terrace
and look at the fields, the trees, read a bit, write
things down, watch guests arrive, admire the large
orderly functioning of this establishment, this little
industry functioning so neatly in the middle of the
countryside, one of thousands all doing the same,
offering food and shelter to travellers, to the best of
its ability.

We eat an enormous dinner, having had just a
sandwich for lunch: *baguette jambon buerre*, half a
French loaf with ham, Bayonne raw ham, and butter; I love this habit of having butter with ham. That
word, enormous, again, maybe it's the country,
ample size seems to be a given. Beginning with *crudités*, superb fresh vegetables in vinaigrette, slices of
sausage, some pâté — because of the meats, it's a
dish of *crudités riches*. Cosmo has *sole meunière*, I *tru-
ite aux amandes*; roast guinea fowl, roast quail, with a
delicious and delicate cauliflower gratin; thin slices
of local cheese, creamy sheep cheese, then home-
made *framboise* which is raspberry ice-cream for
Cosmo and for me a gorgeous peach and an apricot.
The fish is good, the trout excellent; I imagine it
coming out of a nearby mountain stream. The
roasted birds a bit boarding house, thoroughly
cooked, in a brown and sticky gravy. It's probably
better not to think how they produce this variety of

food for hardly any people; the freezer has to come into it.

Instead we go for a walk in the late twilight under the rows of trees in the garden. The six-year-old son of Madame (her husband does the cooking) is sitting on a large plastic tractor with a small wooden bladeless mower attached, pedalling up and down. He's busy, he shouldn't really be spending time talking to us, he can't go to bed until it's really dark, he has all this mowing to finish before he can go to bed.

CRUDITES

These are so good it is always worth mentioning them, possibly because they are mostly forgotten in favour of antipasto. Their name has little to do with the current English notion of the word crudity, being connected to the word *cru*, meaning raw; so is the English word originally but it's gone in the direction of being unrefined, undigested, indigestible, undeveloped, coarse, lacking sophistication, all things which *crudités* aren't.

Basically it's a number of dressed raw vegetables: a fine carrot salad, some sliced tomatoes with possibly a little garlic, a *céleri-rémoulade*, some thin rounds of cucumber, some fennel, strips of red pepper, all these in a simple vinaigrette. Celery. A few olives. Some *cornichons*, the small, crisp unsugared gherkins that put you off the big soggy sweet kind forever. Radishes, with butter and salt. Broad beans, if they are young, for people to shell themselves. Some fresh-cooked beetroot, which stretches the idea of rawness. Whatever you happen to have, and not all of these at once, just a selection, of soft, crisp, spicy. The dressing in France would usually not be olive oil, and mustard would be part of it; I always use olive oil, and sometimes mustard. You can use the same dressing for all the salads, the important thing is to keep the vegetables separate, they must not be mishmashed together.

For *crudités riches* add some slices of salami, and a bit of pâté.

I keep mentioning a simple vinaigrette. I make mine by putting a dash of vinegar in the salad bowl and pouring in quite a lot of good olive oil; I keep a variety, from thick green to pale gold, French, Italian, Spanish, Greek. Sometimes walnut oil. If you want more precise quantities, no more than one part of vinegar to five of oil. (Some people say one to three but I find that far too vinegary; the vinegar is there just as a small sharp note of relief to the oil. On tomatoes, for instance, you don't need any at all. And you could use a little lemon or lime juice.) You can beat in some mustard, say a teaspoon, pepper, salt if you like it. And add a little sweet onion (salad onion, the red Spanish kind or the big white ones) finely chopped. Or some garlic, if it suits. I like to make it fresh in the bowl for each salad; I don't think it's improved by being mixed and kept.

EN PENSION

There were quite a few people in the restaurant but only us dining *à la carte*. The rest were *en pension*, getting breakfast, dinner and bed for a quite cheap price. For dinner they had some sort of veal dish and the cauliflower gratin, three courses to our five. Mostly they drank water, or if wine a small glass and putting the cork back for next time. A couple could make a bottle last three meals at this rate of drinking.

And why are these people, all elderly couples and judging from their cars quite prosperous, staying on guest-house terms at the Béarn Bigorre near Pontacq? For the same reason as us: it is fourteen kilometres from Lourdes.

THE BIGGEST PILGRIMAGE OF ALL

But what happened in this little city at the foot of the Pyrenees? Why, for more than 130 years, has the entire world come in crowds to make pilgrimage?

Because one day the holy virgin appeared to a young girl of fourteen years, Bernadette Soubirous. Because Mary, mother of God and mother of all men, has come here, to the hollow in the rock, to remind us of the secret of happiness: poverty, prayer, penitence, the church ...

The pilgrimage to Compostela is cultural and historic as well as religious. As the display in the rest area reminded us. However simply religious the intention of pilgrims, they can't escape these other elements as they pass through churches lovingly decorated to God through the course of centuries. At Lourdes, religion is all.

The guidebook likes to give practical details, facts, figures: small town of 17 000 people, picturesque market, small businesses, rugby team, ordinary parish life; like so many other small towns in south-west France. Small is the significant word.

Yet: each year five million visitors, from 150 countries. Third highest number of hotels in France: 360 of them, and twenty camping grounds. Seven million letters and cards posted each season. Seventy thousand invalids and people with disabilities. The biggest pilgrimage in the world. Much bigger than Compostela. Bigger than Jerusalem, Rome. Bigger even than Mecca.

There aren't figures for the number of souvenirs sold, though the quantity of these available is only less remarkable than their tattiness and tawdriness, and they are the visitor's first source of amazement.

The guidebook reminds us that the Domain of Our Lady of Lourdes is a sacred space. We must dress properly, not smoke, not bring in any domestic animals, avoid all provocative or boisterous attitudes. We are warned: beware of pickpockets, and give nothing to beggars, there is an aid service for the truly needy. And doubtless experts to decide who they are.

We park the car in a multi-storey car park and emerge into throngs of people and souvenir shops.

Their level of kitsch is awesome. I buy a glittering fridge magnet of the Virgin, very clever, she radiates blue and silver metal ridges of light that seem to pulse as you look at her and all for a couple of dollars, plus a small blue and white plastic madonna with a screw top, it's in fact her crown, for filling with Lourdes water. You can get containers of all sizes from my tiny one to enormous jerrycans.

We pass through streets consisting of nothing but souvenir shops with an occasional café, down towards the Domain. A wide path called the Esplanade comes curving up the hill from the vast spaces in front of the church, whose architecture is very fancy but doesn't catch the attention at all. About as moving as an iced cake at an Easter Show. Great horseshoe steps and paths supported on arcades lead up to it. But we're still making our way past the souvenir shops, when we become aware that there's a red strip painted on the road, like a carpet for a visiting potentate, and along it is coming a constant procession of wheelchairs and carts, small three-wheeled carriages, blue, with ribbed hoods that can be put up or down, and the carts themselves adjustable as bed or chair. They have a long T-shaped bar in front to pull, and often there's someone pushing as well. These belong to Lourdes, and in front is painted the name of the donor, the parish or organisation or person who gave them. They go at a fair clip, they make you think of rickshaw drivers. A rather desperate haste. Maybe they need the momentum to get up the hill, it's very hilly here on the edge of the Pyrénées. We stand and watch them, this promenade of the sick; somehow the spanking pace, the brisk movements of the attendants, some official looking so it's hard to tell whether they're nuns or nurses, some evidently friends and family, this vigour of pace and movement emphasises the frailty of their patients; mortal, moribund, damaged, they roll past in an energetic and buoyant stream.

It's giving me a funny feeling in my chest, this procession; I feel anxious. All very well to laugh at the kitsch, the ugly souvenirs, but this ... Some people are evidently very sick, others mainly decrepit, you think old age is about to claim them and a good thing too. There is a group of youngish people with Down's syndrome and others with wasting diseases; people without legs or arms; one woman with no limbs at all. Perhaps the anxiety I feel is the anxiety of these people, the anxiety of hope, exhaled with every breath, that for *me* a miracle will happen, all praying that the statistical likelihood of blessing will fall upon them; maybe it is the colliding of so many hopes that buffets the air and presses into my chest.

The secretariat has photographs of the extraordinary cures which have taken place; at least three times a week in the season you can go to a *conférence-débat* on the miracles. Since Catherine Latapie, on 1 March 1888, plunged her paralysed hand into the spring brought newly gushing from the mud by the fourteen-year-old Bernadette, there have been thousands of miracles registered by the Medical Bureau, though out of prudence the Church has recognised only sixty-five of them as officially miraculous.

When we get to the actual grotto which is in a cliff under and behind the church, the cave with its pious marble madonna and turrets of candles, there's a huge crowd waiting around with wheelchairs, the carts seem to have gone, the wheelchairs are queueing up to go into the grotto, which is quite shallow; they wait in a sort of massed queue, there's room because the river has been moved to make more space, they wait to go up a little ramp, heaved over by attendants, round through the grotto, keeping up the speed, out. Some touch the wall. A constant procession. An assembly line of wheelchairs. Waiting for the particular one that Our Lady of Lourdes is going to strike well again.

The statue's marble has a shine to it that seems more than usually glabrous, her eyes roll heavenward, she carries a rosary as large and weighty-looking as a prisoner's chain. There are gold roses on her feet. When Bernadette was shown this statue she said, 'It's her, and it's not her.' Poor Bernadette. A pity that the carver of Rocamadour's black madonna wasn't on hand. The pretty sloppy blue and white sentimentality of a million plaster images might have been avoided, and her grotto graced by a slender powerful spine-shivering young woman — the undersized fourteen-year-old girl that Bernadette saw. The first person who ever called her *vous*. Smiling with the compassion and the mystery of God in the corners of her lips …

Hanging up outside the grotto are some five antique and corroded crutches, presumably left behind by the cured. The same ones were there when Cosmo was a student.

I wonder how people imagine God will choose. How he will pick one out of this hopeful stream. With perfect randomness? Or choosing the best prayer? Does anyone really believe He will make limbs grow, restore the elderly to youth? Or that He should? This bothers me: why should He? Cosmo gets harangued by these questions. What do people expect of God, I ask. Isn't it immoral, to demand of Him that He choose you and ignore everyone else? I say the same thing to Nancy when I get back to Australia. It's not like that, says Nancy. People don't go for miracles. It's for an experience of grace. A true pilgrimage. Healing is not what it's about. Healthy people go, says Carol. Worship is perhaps a word to use. Opening yourself to the love that is offered. Spiritual refreshment is mentioned. People going for a holiday, good word, holiday, having this special communion with all the others there.

Quite likely all these things are true. Nevertheless, Lourdes is making me feel quite ill. My head's aching, my shoulders are stiff, my stomach churns. We stop at the taps by the grotto, a pipe and a whole lot of little brass taps conveying the spring water, quite ordinary water, quite simple, no special minerals, no useful curative qualities like the waters of Bourbon l'Archambault or Salies-de-Béarn. Its importance is not in its constitution, but as a sign. I fill my little madonna bottle, among the people with their buckets and jars and jerrycans, and we walk back up the hill, no more carts zipping along, past the souvenir shops to the car park, beside the Cinéma Bernadette, with its continual screening of the story of the child who started it all.

The movie is called *Song of Bernadette*, and has its own legend. In 1940, when Vichy France was collaborating with the Nazis, a novelist named Franz Werfel took refuge in the basilica of Our Lady at Lourdes. Apparently he said if he escaped, he'd dedicate his next book to the saint. The book and the film are the result.

It's said to be rather a good film, with Jennifer Jones, Vincent Price, and Gladys Cooper, as well as Linda Darnell, unbilled, as the Virgin Mary. It won four Oscars, including cinematography for Arthur Miller, and best actress.

I looked up Bernadette in my name book. It's quite commonly given to girls in Catholic families, but actually it's to do with bears; meaning something like 'bear-strong'. It's been popular in Switzerland, Scandinavia, and the Pyrénées, all countries with a lot of bears. They were considered sacred and there are many legends about them. But parents who call their daughters Bernadette are thinking of the young Soubirous and her visions and not of bears.

In the car park is an elderly couple eating a picnic by the boot of their car; they have little folding seats and an Esky and are eating sandwiches in this ugly place where cars go sliding up and down and the air is full of fumes. This is a last straw of sad sights; can't wait to be out of here.

May our life be a pilgrimage, says my pamphlet, a trusting march towards the chapel, the church, the holy city which God is preparing for us and where he waits for us.

And so we set off to St Bertrand de Comminges: church and chapel indeed but quite another story.

ST BERTRAND DE COMMINGES

This town is in the middle of the chain of mountains that forms the Pyrénées, halfway between the Atlantic and the Mediterranean, up in the foothills. As you drive towards it you can see its cathedral high up ahead, like a great ship sailing. It was built in Romanesque style but wasn't big enough for the enormous number of pilgrims passing through, so most of it is Gothic extension, finishing in a tall square tower with wooden boards round a pointed pyramid roof. This is Ste Marie de Comminges, in the town of St Bertrand de Comminges.

It's hot midday when we arrive, the sort of heat that sends you skittering across the cobbles to shelter in narrow edges of shade. The way into the church, the main part, is through the cloister; you pay at a little box office. Cloisters are always moving, but this one ... your eyes water with the beauty of it. It's built on the edge of a steep ravine. Three of its sides are Romanesque with round arches, the fourth against the church is Gothic. There are columns with *entrelacs* in the form of basket work, leaves, figures. Cloisters are about enclosed spaces but here the side away from the church is open to the valley, so you look through the arches and the great rectangular windows beyond, across and down into the thickly wooded ravine which, according to a notice on the church's wooden lavatories, real dunnies these, was a home for the Maquis; the Resistance hid in this difficult terrain. Today the air trembles with the rich green light of summer. Cloisters invite you to contemplate them, to stand and gaze … at their straight lines, their repeated arches, their decoration that St Bernard criticised so lovingly. And this one offers as well that fall of deeply forested valley that has been and not just once the scene of passionate and bloody struggle, now imbued with a peace as palpable as the green light that fills it. Maybe it always was, which is why it was a good spot for the Resistance.

This is perhaps the most beautiful cloister I've seen. Moissac? More powerful perhaps. Lofty. Grand. This is intimate, and simple. But all cloisters are simple, apparently, and deceptively, they have that satisfying repetition which belongs to the rhythm of natural things like trees and flowers and can only be achieved by the most scrupulous art, so that you forget it's there.

Inside the church is a lot of Renaissance wood carving which is wicked and knowing and full of jokes and licentiousness: a stall with its misericord of a woman with wings and bird's talon feet and a bearded face where her private parts would be — whatever was the feeling of a monk who rested his own bum on that? A free-standing Adam and Eve,

Eve holding the apple to her chest like a third breast, the snake half woman, trees with marvellous wooden fruit — this carver is keen on apples and breasts and mixes them up. More misericords, with faces full of malice, spite, anguish, sly smiles. There are sixty-six of these carved choir stalls, shining brown and polished: worth the entrance fee.

L'OPPIDUM

We have lunch at a restaurant in one of those frequent excellent finely run small town hotels, called l'Oppidum, which Cosmo says means fortified town. As of course you can see St Bertrand de Comminges still is, with its ramparts and narrow gates. With a long and glorious as well as bloody past, since it was founded in 76 BC by the great Pompey. He called it Lugdunum Convenarum, it was part of the Province Narbonnaise. Four years after the death of Christ, Herod, Tetrarch of Galilee, and his wife Herodias, the one who made her daughter Salome ask for the head of John the Baptist in reward for her dancing, were exiled here by the Emperor Caligula. This seems to be fact, not medieval wishful thinking.

Just outside the town there are archaeological sites, uncovering the ruins of Roman baths, a theatre, a forum, a temple and a fourth-century Christian basilica. After Roman times, when its population was 60 000, the town had some quiet moments but also periods that were seriously eventful: sieges, battles, tyrannies, treacheries, and the saint who gave it his name. Even that went at one stage; the revolution took away its ecclesiastical privileges and called it Hauteville: Hightown. My elderly guidebook says, 'Eventually it resumed its glorious name, but is no more than a village crushed by its past.'

Not any more. Not crushed. History invigorates. There's a constant bunching of tourists. And people, mostly young, cherishing its heritage. As well as a marvellous organ, which makes it a centre of summer music festivals. We buy some cassettes of this organ playing Bach and listen to them in the car. The music, the gorgeously carved organ, even the mighty cathedral itself, are all flying heavenward. Turn around and look up at it from the valley below. It's lifting off.

But first, lunch. We take the eighty franc menu. St Bertrand has entirely cured us of Lourdes and we're starving. To begin with, *chèvre avec pommes*: a mustardy lettuce salad, slices of toasted baguette, with a half apple roasted, and on it a slice of goat's cheese, the kind that has a rind. All hot and sprinkled with caraway seed, the rind keeping the melted cheese from running away. Delicious, excellent combination of flavours. So we say to the woman serving, Ah, is this a speciality of the region, or is it a speciality of the chef? No, not the region, it's the chef's idea, he got it out of a low cholesterol cookbook.

We undo that with the next course. Though I didn't have duck hearts on a skewer, which was probably a bit cowardly of me. We eat *côtes d'agneau en brochette*, which are three each very tender very small pink lamb chops which have been marinated in herbs, threaded on a skewer and grilled on an open fire. Cosmo has lemon meringue tart and I *Paris-Brest*, both fairly solid but honest cakes. Lemon meringue pie is on the menu of the next hotel we stay in, so perhaps it is a speciality of the region. I'm putting it here anyway, and remembering how good were the lemon meringue pies my mother used to make.

LEMON MERINGUE PIE

Make a pastry using 150 g flour and 125 g butter, mixed with a little cold water. You can increase the amount of butter to make the pastry crisp and buttery, but too much and it won't roll out easily. Fill a pie dish, and bake blind in a 190°C oven.

Filling: Measure 275 mL water. Mix 3 tablespoons cornflour and 50 g of sugar in a bowl, add enough of the water to make a smooth paste. Put the rest of the water and grated rind of two lemons into a saucepan, boil, pour on to cornflour paste and mix till smooth. Put back in the saucepan, boil, then simmer gently, stirring, for a minute. Take off heat and beat in 3 egg yolks, the juice of the lemons, and 40 g butter. Fill pastry case.

Meringue: Beat the whites of the eggs to form stiff peaks. Add 100 g caster sugar, beating in a quarter at a time. Spread over lemon filling, to cover completely. Bake in the oven at 150°C until lightly browned and set on the outside, for 45 minutes or an hour.

If your freezer has some spare egg whites you could increase the number to 4 or 5, increasing the sugar a little too, for a higher meringue.

St Just

Down the hill from St Bertrand is another church, the basilica of St Just de Valcabrère, set in a graveyard, entirely Romanesque, eleventh century, but incorporating various old tombstones, several from the year 347, and on the gateway to the cemetery an inscription in stone belonging to the first century. The altar was consecrated in 1200 to St Etienne, first martyr, and to St Just and St Pasteur, Spanish martyrs decapitated in 304. The relics of Just and Pasteur were kept in a tomb on the altar, and there's a double staircase curving round on either side of it, so that pilgrims could climb up and touch the reliquary. And underneath the sarcophagus is a small vaulted passage, so that people could pray under their protection. I've mentioned how important relics were in pilgrim churches; without them nobody would stop there, even if the food was good, and people went to great lengths to steal a saint if that was the only way to get hold of them, like St Helena in Champagne. Conques is another example: the food wasn't much anyway, and with no relics nobody would come. So a monk was sent to Agen to steal the bones of the child martyr St Foy; it took him ten years to get into a position of trust so he could make off with the relics, which were very closely guarded, but when he did get hold of them the saint seemed pleased, she made a small fog so that the monk could elude capture, and performed a number of miracles in her new home, which ensured lots of pilgrims and raised plenty of money for the monks to begin building a magnificent church, and then of course they could ask for lots of donations to this end; thus Conques established itself as a place on the pilgrim route.

The tympanum of St Just has friendly carvings of Christ in majesty, surrounded by homely chubby apostles sporting their symbols, and by the door are column statues, three beardless youths holding books, presumably the church's saints, and a woman with a cross. They are standing on crouched animals like people on a tomb, and still show signs of the colours they were originally painted.

The church is made of golden stone, set in fields dried golden by the golden sun, its roofs are rosy terracotta, and inside its graveyard walls are rows of dark green poplars. It's hard to imagine the ancient grim history these places have lived through, except that the sun and the fields and the distant ancestors of these trees would have looked just the same a millennium ago: peaceful, timeless.

SAINT GIRONS

We spend the night in this town at a one-star high bourgeois establishment called the Hôtel Eychenne. It's grander than we need but we're too tired to keep looking. An old posting inn with a gravel courtyard where we can park the car and a good show of geraniums. Our room looks across it to the kitchens, which are full of young people in white clothes waiting for the evening to begin. They smoke, and play cards, drink water and laugh softly in the lazy late afternoon time before the work of dinner. The kitchen is smooth and gleaming, everything is suspended as they wait for their customers to come and eat.

There aren't in fact many of us, and most are English couples with no conversation. The two next to us have a fight over her duck, it's breast and comes rare, she can't stand it. When the headwaiter sees she hasn't eaten it he offers to bring something else, but she won't have it. Her husband is angry, he hisses that of course they would have thought she knew what she was doing when she ordered it, of course duck breast is always pink, of course everyone knows that. He's probably thinking of how much it cost. They sit tense with anger, not speaking, seething. The gloomy atmosphere is not pleasant, especially as Cosmo and I have plenty to talk about, perhaps surprising considering we're rarely out of one another's sight, even in the bathroom. We're only apart in public lavatories. On this occasion we recall the story that Michael Symons told me, about a battle between Philip Searle and Patrick White, over the same thing, rare duck. White said, Well done, Searle said not in his restaurant. It was Possums in Adelaide. White said he would have duck, and he would have it well done. He thumped his stick. His titanic will menaced the man who was there to serve him. Searle said, No way. I forget who won, Searle I think.

All the silent couples finish much earlier than us, so we take the last of our wine which for a change is a classy one and needs savouring out into the courtyard and sit in the cool twilight to finish it.

The meal wasn't great: good *moules marinières* for Cosmo, and I had *palourdes et coques*, small clams and pipis, which were wonderfully garlicky, then *chateaubriand* and for me veal which was disappointing: *escalope de veau à la crème*, and I had it because it's so hard to find real veal in Australia. This was a thick slab of yearling which would have displeased anywhere, far too thick and meaty, and the sauce too demi-glaze and overwrought and boring. Good vegetable, a sort of ratatouille in slices, and for dessert *crème brulée Catalan*. I asked the waitress how it was different from normal *crème brulée* and she said not at all, it was just the name. It was a proper one, rich cream, not too solid, and a thin thin coating of toffee. Cosmo had *croustades de Cousaren*, a flakey apple pastry, a local dish.

SLOW MORNING

We don't get up very early or pack up very fast. Yesterday we did a lot. And ate two large meals: good while it was happening but not good for us. We feel quite sluggish. I sit at a table in the flowery courtyard and do some writing. Lourdes is a long way away. What I remember is St Bertrand, and St Just. Thinking of them I can recapture how moved I felt. Still do. The calm valleys and these mighty works.

Maybe if I'd been around when these medieval constructions were new I'd have been disturbed by them as by Lourdes: made nervous, anxious, looked at the pilgrims and doubted. Is it simply time that has got rid of their anguish? No — it's beauty.

ST LIZIER

We go back several kilometres from St Girons in order to see St Lizier, which is a fortified town on top of a hill, important in Roman times. The cathedral is eleventh century and it shows how the process of heritage rescue is flourishing in France. The thirty-year-old guidebook describes it briefly, but since then some frescos have been discovered, which are in excellent condition in parts, though not altogether. There's a thirteenth-century Christ in majesty with a face like a lion, a slightly puzzled lion, and some figures that are older still, including a visitation done before 1117. The figures of Mary and her cousin Elizabeth, the two pregnant women, are patchy but full of life, and the colours are exquisite, a marvellous rose-terracotta and a turquoisy blue. Paintings as old as these in damp mouldering stone churches are rare; these must have been quite well preserved by whatever it was that covered and hid them.

There are big vases of roses everywhere, the church is scented with roses. At midday a bell rings, not striking the time, simply ringing midday. And there's a cloister full of sunlight, unusual for being two storeys high. Under its arches is an exhibition on easels, photographs and text, scholarly and fascinating, tracing the movement of images in religious art between the Adriatic and the Atlantic, pagan, Christian and Muslim, from Roman to Renaissance times, through Italy, France, Spain. I wish it was in a book I could buy, there's not time to read it closely now. Though enough to notice some juxtapositions: painted heads from Pompeii beside those of St Lizier; amazing correspondences.

There's an antique shop by the church door, and we get into conversation with its owner. She's eighty-seven, she tells us, and keeps going for the interest of it; she loves talking and it's hard to get away. She brings out some old fabrics to show us, sixteenth century, seventeenth, gorgeous things.

On top of the hill is the old episcopal palace, inside a wall whose ramparts have Roman foundations. We drive in and manage to have a good look at it before somebody comes and shouts that we have no right to be here, it's shut. It's got a panorama. At last we see the Pyrénées, and it's at this late moment we realise how massively they've been there all along. All this time they've been accompanying us, and we didn't know. These looming peaks with their shining brilliant snow, invisible. Perhaps you need winter and clear cold air to see them properly. This weather is so hot and sunny and seems bright but the air is hazy. Maybe all the moisture in it is why nobody wears any protection against the sun. Yesterday we saw a woman driving a tractor through the sun-baked dusty fields wearing a swimsuit and shorts, nothing else, no hat.

LOST SAINTS

We've stayed in the town of St Girons, whose church is St Valier, we've been to the cathedral of St Lizier. Back down the road is St Gaudens and its neighbour St Marcet. A few days ago we were tempted by the road to St Plaisir. Who are these saints?

Later I look them up in various books but can find no mention of them. Cosmo says that these are the saints who simply didn't make it into the canon. They were martyrs, they performed holy deeds, their lives were miraculous, they were just as important in their day as those we still remember. St Catherine, St Barbara, St Lucy; St Jerome, St Vincent, St Hubert, St Vitus: none of these was necessarily more significant, stronger or more wonderful in their faith, they were just lucky, they didn't get forgotten. Their stories kept being told. The others slipped through the cracks of history. I think of places round Sévérac: St Come, St Geniez, St Chély, St Cernin. Some of the names may be corruptions of famous ones — St Geniez might be Genesius — but most of them exist only in these mysterious place names. How accidental it all is. And rather sad. I'd like to know who St Lizier was. A man or a woman. People say 'and their name lives on' but a name all by itself is a funny kind of immortality, if nobody knows who you were.

THE SUN

We couldn't be bothered having breakfast at the hotel, the people were supercilious and the coffee extravagantly dear. We mean to have coffee somewhere but don't come across anywhere so we stop for lunch at Rimont, in the shady garden of le Bouquet de Provence, with its view across the valley. We have sandwiches made of *pain*, not baguette, so more than twice as fat. Cosmo has pâté with *cornichons* and I have *saucisson*, lovely meaty thick slices. I do like sandwiches when they're good.

Walking across the square from the shade of the trees to where the car's parked, I think about the sun and how hot it is, but how it's a profitable heat, that gets into wine, and honey, and vegetables, and lavender and all the things that grow in this part of the world. Cheese, says Cosmo, but I'm not sure about sun and cheese; grass into milk, I suppose.

But you can see how the earth loves the sun. It's benign.

At Foix we have some coffee, in a café that has its tables set up under a lofty covered market. Some young women with babies set up beside us, and have conversations with the waitress, who's a friend. The mothers seem about fifteen, but that's probably my problem. It's a busy little town, all the parking places full. We can see a large fortified castle in good order, with towers and keeps and Gallo-Roman fortifications (well, we take these on trust) close by, on a small peak in the middle of the valley, we look at it as we drink short blacks and long waters; looking is enough. A feudal castle with a romantic silhouette, says the guidebook. Yes indeed, looking is enough.

Though we do call in to le Poujols because a road sign tells us there's a fortified church. Very plain bare end with machicolations and a superb *tour peigne* (a tower in the shape of a comb) with bells between the teeth and fairy lights around the crenellations. Beside it is a hairy man lying on a banana bed in his front garden, soaking up the sun. The village is shuttered up against the heat; two women are sitting in a strip of shade on their doorstep trying to get cool. We ask them do they know what the temperature is. It was supposed to be thirty, they say, and storms.

It feels hotter than that.

We stop again at Mirepoix: I knew the culinary term but not that it was named after a town. It's the mixture of diced onion, carrot, celery, with some ham and herbs, gently stewed together to form the basis of certain dishes: braises, casseroles, sauces. It's actually named after a person, the Duke of Mirepoix, who was fond of it. Mirepoix is a good place on a hot day, it has a pretty garden square surrounded by fifteenth- and sixteenth-century houses. On the ground level are wide pavements, which are overhung by the first storey, it actually projects the width of the pavement, so you can walk in shady cool arcades. The buildings are half-timbered and prettily painted, and the massive wooden beams that support the first floors are some of them carved with fanciful faces. It's a place you come upon with surprise and delight. The geraniums are excellent.

CRAGS AND CLIFFS
AND DEEP STONE WALLS

The walls at the castle of Foix have Gallo-Roman foundations, third century in fact. So does St Lizier. The town that is now St Bertrand de Comminges was founded by Pompey a century just about before Christ. Carcassonne is much the same age, first a Roman stronghold protecting the route from the Mediterranean to the Altlantic, then Visigoth, then Frankish. Others are younger but no less strong. Lastours' four sister fortresses occupy a site that was important in prehistoric times, on a crag 165 metres wide and some 1300 metres long. Mirepoix is not a mountain eyrie, but was a walled township, a *bastide*. Villages were fortified, and so were farms.

Not to mention churches. Wars of every kind raged up and down these valleys: Roman conquests, barbarian invasions, neighbourly disputes, feudal struggles, skirmishes with the Spanish, wars of occupation like the English, dynastic disagreements, wars of religion. This must be some of the most disputed territory in the world. And at the same time, anciently civilised.

NOTES FOR THE BESIEGED

What do you do when your town is being besieged? When you are trapped inside your city's walls with an army encamped outside, maybe bombarding you, certainly waiting till you starve, or begin to die of thirst?

You take your last pig, or cow, or goat. And your last bag of grain. You feed the one to the other, then hurl the animal from your ramparts into the midst of the besiegers. The beast bursts open, and the besiegers are dumbfounded. So, you have so much food you can afford to waste it in this way? It's evident that you can hold out a great while, the siege is obviously doomed.

Disheartened, the besiegers pack up and go away.

There are a number of variants on this story, but mostly it's the last beast and the last bushel of grain, though one version has an eagle dropping a big fat trout inside a beleaguered city, which the inhabitants toss over the wall, providing evidence of such a cavalier attitude to food that the sitting army gives up. The most famous version is told of Carcassonne. Its ruler Dame Carcas was having trouble with Charlemagne. It was a sow stuffed with wheat that she cast among his men. It burst and sprayed everybody with grain. The Francs were stunned at the sight of such waste, and concluded that a mad abundance reigned in the city still.

When Charlemagne packed up and went away Dame Carcas blew victory trumpets: *Carcas sonne*, people said; Carcas is sounding her trumpets. So giving the city its name.

It all sounds something like an urban myth to me. The legend of Dame Carcas comes out of one of the *Chansons de Geste* which always have an imaginative way with the facts, but the Dame is alive and well in contemporary Carcassonne. You can eat in her restaurant and see her statue and find her name invoked in antique lettering for all sorts of commercial purposes.

I'm intrigued by this siege story, by the way the ploy always seemed to work, up and down the centuries. Nobody ever seemed to notice it had been done before. Nobody seemed to wonder why people would toss overfed cows and pigs over ramparts even if they had more than they knew what to do with. Nobody seemed to suspect that it might be a trick. Dispirited besiegers always seemed to decamp.

Other siege stories are grimmer. Less legend and more harsh fact. Especially those relating to the religious and civil wars, the crusades against the heretic Cathars. The town of Minerve was fortified by nature, and by walls built on its sheer cliffs, but had only one well, at the base of a towering cliff, reached by a small fortified stairway. Simon de Montfort bombarded the stairs, using a huge catapult set on the other side of the ravine. Finally, thirst in that hot summer of 1210 forced the Minervois to surrender. One hundred and forty Cathars were burned to death — many throwing themselves into the flames of their own volition. A year later, at Lavaur, three or four hundred Cathars were burned, and another Dame, Guirande, thrown into a well and buried under stones. Eighty knights had their throats slit. In 1209, the people of Béziers were invited to save themselves by handing over the Cathars within the city, but they refused. The crusaders made a surprise attack, and massacred the inhabitants, Cathars and Catholics, indiscriminately. The leader of the crusaders is supposed to have said: Slay them all. God will recognise his people.

The foothills of the Pyrénées are strung with Cathar castles, massive ruins most of them, built on great rocky outcrops. The stones of men grow out of the stones of nature in a way that is forbidding, and foreboding, yet organic; you marvel at the might of them, at the conception of these great walls of stone growing out of mountains of rock, at the engineering skills, and at the labour of the men involved. How could they even climb up there, let alone build walls out of huge blocks of stone. I bet no record was ever kept of those who perished in making these castles.

When they were new they must have been terrifying places, and dreadful deeds were done in them. Simon de Montfort cut off the noses, ears, and lips of a group of prisoners and gouged out their eyes, except for one man who was left with one eye so he could lead them to Lastours to persuade the castle to surrender. These fortresses are still, in the pleasant summer countryside and all overgrown with green, still forbidding, and full of melancholy. You think you ought to hate them for the evil that happened here, but you don't, they're beautiful and somehow moving. Maybe their charm is the contrast between bloodiness and the serenity of nature. Except that maybe the bloodiness is like the castles an extension of what's already there. Hidden in nature. Maybe there's an excitement in ancient crimes which is safe: fascinating but not threatening.

Perhaps it's a palpable manifestation of the Cathar doctrine of Dualism. How could a merciful God have created Evil, when He Himself is Goodness infallible? A hard question that has troubled Christians from the beginning, and for which the Cathars found an answer, and not a bad one: there is one God, the God of Good, and then there is Evil, a lower principle that created the World. Salvation means freeing yourself from the world of Evil and reaching the kingdom of Good. Striving for perfection by discarding the pleasures of the flesh, and not having children who'll keep the sinful world going. The Cathars weren't afraid of death because for them hell was on earth. That's why they jumped into the flames.

One etymological theory is that the Cathars came from Bulgaria; they were Bulgars. The kind of sex they practised in order not to have children was given their name and provides our word buggery, from bugger, Bulgar.

They seem to have been gentle people, loving, thoughtful, spiritual, practising a very pure — the name means pure — and rather idiosyncratic kind of Christianity which the rest of Catholic France decided was heresy, for reasons of power, not of holiness. The result was that for the Cathars hell was indeed created on earth.

The Catholics did try to convert them, or at least get some nominal recantation, but the Cathars would have none of it. You could say that the fortresses in which they took refuge when persecuted remain today symbols of freedom defended to the death.

The war against the Cathars was called the Albigensian Crusade, after the town of Albi; it began as a military effort on the Church's part to put down the heresy, but it ended up as a struggle for political power, for who owned this southern part of France. The Cathars lost so thoroughly that their conquerors believed every trace was wiped out. Still the idea of them remains, powerful historically and certainly touristically. But though it's a heritage exploited for its cultural tourism there are deeper and perhaps more nourishing meanings. So that people may understand their present by considering their past.

There are plenty of books, from guidebooks to scholarly works, about the Cathars. Even the signposts remember them, pointing to their strong-holds, their towns and castles, so many of them that this part of Languedoc is called Cathar country. So much for trying to deny them their name and history.

I am a tourist in this present moment; this is not my country, I did not come from here, my ancestors were not of this land. But the past is a different matter; there are ways in which it belongs to me, ways in which I am no more a tourist in its tortuous paths than anyone else who chooses to become part of it by contemplating it.

CAMPING

Carcassonne may be the place where Dame Carcas blew her trumpets to celebrate the frustration of Charlemagne, it may be the derelict city which Viollet-le-Duc restored with excessive zeal, say some, creating a Disney-smooth vision of pepper-pot-towered perfection, out of his comfortable nineteenth-century certainty. But there's a certain Carcassonne that belongs to me, a Carcassonne of happy memory.

The kids were two years old, and five, and we were camping. On a tight budget as we always were in France, or anywhere, for that matter. We'd borrowed a tent from friends, which was for two people, with a bedroom and a kind of annexe. We'd borrowed their tables and chairs and camping-gaz stove and lantern, too. Cosmo and I slept in the car, a Peugeot 504 with a camping body. Our joke was that a person needed a camping body to sleep in such a car; there was a definite knack to it, getting your hips and knees and neck in the right place. Definitely an activity for people whose bones are young and supple.

The woman who took our money when we arrived at the camping ground in Carcassonne said she was making *bouillabaisse* and we could have some if we wanted. I think Cosmo went over and got it, later; anyway, there was a good helping, hot in an aluminium saucepan and we ate it with great enthusiasm; it was very good. Goodness knows how authentic, this far from the Mediterranean, but tasting great. Various sorts of fish, and a lot of garlic, and some potatoes, all yellow with saffron. I remember we put the pot on the ground, a solid old battered pot it was, after we'd scraped it out, and a cat came and licked it, which pleased the children. They were great eaters, you could take them anywhere and feed them anything.

Camping was hard work, with all the gear we had to carry, packing it in and out of the car, and James was still in nappies, the itinerant life making for slow toilet training. I remember this effort well, but I also remember how idyllic it was, and how I knew at the time that it was. We had a green *Michelin* guide to camping and always picked the best places with hot water and good toilets, as well as trees and particular beauties for the eye, like rivers or lakes, and close to significant sites. We'd arrive late in the afternoon and the kids would play on the swings (we'd chosen those from the guide too) while we put up the tent, always complicated with its metal poles to slot together, and then we'd cook the food we'd bought, I remember I'd got a pot of basil in Arles and used to sit in the car with it between my feet for safety, so often I'd buy lamb and courgettes and aubergines and tomatoes to go with it, and we'd eat and talk and the kids would be put to bed and we'd sit in the calm cool peace of a country evening and have another glass of wine and talk more about what we'd done and would do, and go to bed ourselves and read by the lights in the car. Then wriggle our hips into place and sleep the sleep of the virtuously tired.

In Carcassonne I remember waking up early, not quite dawn though the night was fading, and Cosmo waking too and us making love, aware that people nearby were up and packing for an early start, Spanish I think they were speaking, and that the car was rocking, and trying to make love without moving much and not succeeding and not caring either, and getting up and walking across wet grass and having hot showers and eating breakfast and packing and being up at the town gate when it opened to let the tourists in. Buying some postcards and eating another breakfast while we wrote on the cards of the fairybook city to send home: dear granny and grandfather, my parents were still alive then and I was not an orphan, there was another generation to take the ultimate responsibility, whatever that was. Lucy wrote her full name in red biro on the card, she'd just learnt how. This day was known for quite some time as the day we had two breakfasts.

The restored ramparts have a pathway that runs along just below the battlements, and we walked along this, on a tour, the guide offering all sorts of interesting facts. He pointed out that this walkway killed more people than the enemy; one careless step backwards and you fell five or ten or twenty metres and that was the end of you. You might be lucky enough to die instantly. I was carrying James, a strong healthy well-grown two-year-old who didn't want to be carried. This was in the time when I seemed to spend an inordinate amount of time preventing this intrepid child from killing himself. I still do worry about him killing himself but I can no longer do anything about it.

I had great difficulty keeping him hoisted on my hip; he wanted to explore. I could see him going the same way as the briefly thoughtless soldiers. That same year we were in England, at a theatre, in the front row of the gods, watching *Peter Pan*. Dorothy Tutin was playing this role, and flew about the stage in a dramatic manner. Nana the dog had barely appeared when the curtain dropped down and a man came out front and asked us to leave, quickly and quietly. It was urgent, he said. James was having none of that. He hung on to the velvet rail of the balcony, drummed his feet against my legs, and roared. I had to prise him off, several times, because he'd latch back on again, and carry him, still yelling and kicking in his sturdy leather shoes against my shins, down flight after flight of concrete stairs, my own legs trembling so much I didn't know how I could walk on them. Lucy went docilely down, and fast, being a sensible older sister. I had James round the middle, face outwards, all the struggling and him being so heavy anyway making me unsure how long I could hold on to him. I thought it might be a fire and we would be trapped. James didn't care, he wanted to see the play, he was beside himself with rage at being taken away so soon.

We stood on the pavement on the other side of the road. No smoke, no flames. A bomb scare, the Irish, so rumour ran round after a bit. It was grey London midwinter. We had to wait hours before being let in again. James went back to the red velvet rail of the gods as to a right. I only had to hang on to him constantly so he didn't climb up and pitch over it.

When I had time to think calmly about the whole affair, of course I was pleased that the theatre had aroused such passion in him. I could enjoy his cleverness, even as I felt the tenderness in my shins.

Carcassonne wasn't such a noisy battle as the London theatre, and Cosmo was there to take turns, though I seemed to do better at holding him, something to do with the hip, sitting him on it and clamping him tight so he couldn't get away. I listened to what the guide said, too, and learned a lot about medieval siege warfare.

GOING BACK

You can see your life as a straight line from birth to death, a kind of time line, with notches marking significant events, a firmly ruled line. Or you can see it as a series of loops, turning back on itself, linear still, but forming circles, or ellipses, possibly moving forward as it loops backwards, or perhaps sideways, but not marching ever onward like a Christian soldier. Maybe it's a spiral, the loops higher or lower, upwards or downwards, differently angled. I prefer this view to the ruled straight line.

A pilgrimage may be a journey to a place you haven't been before, for penance, or illumination, or ceremony. But it may also be a return to a place you know, a beloved place, a place of happy memory. The whole reason of a pilgrimage may be just that, a return, and it will have a sacred quality because it is paying attention to the person you once were, it's a celebration and an understanding of something that was in the past important. Part of our turning back from Compostela is the desire to revisit places we have been happy in. A dangerous business, quite possibly, because you might not like it there this next time, you might spoil the old memories. Well, life is a risk at the best of times.

So: to Carcassonne again. A hotel this time, no camping. Inside the walls, so we can take our car in; we explain to the guardian at the gate that we have a booking. This is because Cosmo rang up from Foix. The Hôtel des Remparts, a clean indifferent room looking through a small barred window on to the great well that gives the square its name and the hotel its address — the place du Grand Puits. The hotel has a fabulous winding wide stone staircase — I suspect Viollet-le-Duc. Or his heirs. We walk round in the twilight. I buy a teeshirt because I'm so bored with my hot weather clothes, I was expecting a civilised chilly summer and didn't bring many, it's coral pink with a sketch of pepper-pot towers and very cheap. The classy souvenir shops are beginning to shut. We sit in the place Martou and have a drink; it's a paved area covered with tables, we order some rosé and it comes in a small pitcher, very cold.

The thing to eat in Carcassonne is *cassoulet* (not *bouillabaisse*). We choose the restaurant of Dame Carcas and sit at its outdoor tables ready to order, but the waiter is rude and some buskers start playing on the steps of the fountain beside us so we leave.

Outside our hotel is a billboard advertising the restaurant St Jean. It mentions tomato salad. Suddenly we have an urgent desire to eat tomato salad. The food in the south-west is a bit rich and meaty and makes you wish you were a manual worker; some plain sweet vegetable is seductive. The tomatoes aren't great, not a patch on the ones from Pialligo, the market gardens near the airport in Canberra that nearly disappear every now and then under grandiose schemes for the military or hotels, but the Pialligo tomatoes are straight off the vine, in fact sometimes it's you who has to pick them, their growers have been too busy, and they're available only for several weeks a year. They make you think you should only eat tomatoes when they have been grown within a few kilometres and a few days of where you are.

The Carcassonne ones have decent oil and masses of green and white garlic and good bread to mop them up. We rather wreck the vegetable effect by following them with the ubiquitous *cassoulet*, which is certainly rich and meaty, but at least we have the simple one, beans and pork and sausage, no preserved duck.

We're sitting in the place St Jean, in a curve of the city ramparts, by the side of the castle and the lists, the long grassy spaces where tournaments were held. There's a welcome fresh breeze here. Walled towns can be stuffy. We begin with a glass of sparkling wine, Blanquette de Limoux. Good bubbles. We've been missing sparkling wine on this trip — it sets one up so. Beer is not the same, though it is nourishing after a hot day in fortified villages and Romanesque churches and dusty little cars, but a bit heavy, and not so restorative as a good glass of Australian bubbly. The French don't understand this; champagne is expensive and only for ceremonies and celebrations. The idea of a cheap delicious sparkling wine at the end of a busy day is not familiar. Well, maybe for the very rich. Small shallow glasses of champagne on restaurant menus cost as much as a bottle in Oz, and more.

This Blanquette de Limoux is delicious on a terrace by the lists at Carcassonne, but later when we buy a bottle it seems a bit sweet, not dry and bracing like Australian sparkling wine. Though later again I find out it is the oldest sparkling wine in France, protected by royal decree in 931. Who'd have thought it. I reckon a fortune is to be made by the person who comes up with a good generic name for Aussie bubbly. And markets it as itself, not well-of-course-we-know-it-is-not-as-good-as-the-French champagne.

Our restaurant is new, only two months old; the young men running it are full of ideas. They serve what they call *assiettes*, mixed plates, a bit like the Spanish *platos*, with a number of things, meat, vegetables, salad, cheese, fruit, all together, good for lunch perhaps though I do like three-course meals, they have a sort of logic to them, a satisfying curve, and they take longer. The plates are popular, a lot of people are ordering them. The St Jean seems a place for locals, we notice a number of people from the shops we passed, they've closed up and come to sit in the summer evening and enjoy themselves. In a town full of variously ingenious tourist traps, the integrity of this place must be quite useful.

The sky here is beautiful; we can't see the sunset, but the colours change: orange, and deep rose, violet, pale jade green. Then when it's night the floodlights come on, with their games of darkness and black black shadows.

We have cheese to finish, with a little fat hot bun, Cantal for me and Roquefort for Cosmo. And more of the cold well-flavoured rosé wine in pitchers.

BEER TRUCKS

The morning: looking through our barred window down at the square. The busloads of tourists must have arrived, a number of stoutish elderly parties pottering along, also quite a lot of young people, some of them a bit strange, like metamorphosed hippies, others brash and in master-of-the-universe mode but at least they stop you having the sense that looking at historical France is an activity almost entirely geriatric.

Beside the great well is a truck delivering barrels of beer and cases of bottles. It's hard work in these medieval cities delivering anything; I'm thinking how shocked Australian workers would be by the sort of conditions people have to work under here, which they take for granted, quite cheerfully and extremely noisily. The small old square is like a sound shell. They enjoy dropping barrels on cobblestones, thumping doors, crashing bottles. And they get their vehicles into spaces you wouldn't believe; the gap between the well and the beer truck is tiny but a van has just slithered through it.

I can spend a lot of time looking out a window watching this daily life going on.

We go and find some coffee and a croissant for breakfast, then wander round the town. We decide to give the castle and the tour of the ramparts a miss, there seems rather too much hearty reconstructed simple-minded medievalism around. It may be charming in small doses. I'd rather remember our thoughtful guide of twenty years ago.

Instead we look at the church. The basilica of St Nazaire has ancient beautiful windows and a magnificent organ. Its façade is fortified, from when it was part of the Visigoth wall.

For lunch we go back to the St Jean: appropriate, because this is St Jean's day, St John the Baptist, Midsummer's Day. We eat roast beef and tomato sandwiches with mustard, on some lovely chunky country bread, and set out on the next stage. From the motorway we look back at Carcassonne floating in its sunny haze, ethereal, impossibly romantic. The ruined castles weathering into rock have mass and weight, Carcassonne is whole and insubstantial. Some little painted knights with banners, some ladies with gilded dresses, and you could be looking at a page in a *Book of Hours*.

THE GRUESOME CHOOK

Was it dangerous to come here? We are older now, we don't see the world so freshly, nor does it lie before us, so various, so beautiful, so new, as once it did. There's not the span of time to come that once there was. Our children are grown up, we are not so short of money as we were, we do not have to work so hard at travelling. Our memory of Carcassonne was about being young, and lithe and limber, and being able to cope with babies and nappies and a tent, and dinner not a matter of choosing the right restaurant but buying and cooking it, and survival depending on having enough cash because we had no credit cards, not one. And still, we knew we were lucky simply to be there, and it's the sense of that luckiness that we've remembered.

So yes, of course we are feeling a little bit melancholy. But not regretful. The past belongs to us, we can inhabit it at will, and the present isn't too bad at all. The future … we talk about it a lot, being human, and that's a problem all of us have, always speculating about what's to happen. I like to hang on to the past, the good past, it's safe, it's over, and without it the present, always leaking into the future, is too ephemeral. So middle-aged we walk around Carcassonne. And so do the young parents, with their cheerful squirming son and calmer delighted daughter who knows she's in a picture book; there they all are, sitting at a café table and eating breakfast, they will have eaten two breakfasts that day, and writing postcards to the grandparents.

We bought a faïence plate in the old city, Moustiers, an imitation of course, new, with a pheasant on it, and hung it on the wall in the flat in Paris. What's that gruesome chook doing there, asked James, suddenly, irrelevantly. Of course we laughed, in delight and astonishment; he was two. I packed it badly for travelling home, and it broke. I've still got the pieces, and maybe I'll stick it back together one day. But we don't need the plate, Cosmo and I, to possess the gruesome chook, and the way we laughed.

L'ETANG DE THAU

This is a lagoon, a large body of water scooped in from the Mediterranean, not in Provence but Languedoc. We're making another loop, retracing a visit made ten years ago, and another twenty years before that, in Cosmo's past, before he knew me, when he was still a student. He came here to the wedding of Catherine and Etienne. Her family had a house on the edge of the lagoon with a lawn in front where they'd set up tables covered with white cloths, like a scene from that kind of movie, made by Louis Malle or Claude Chabrol, in which the charming forms of domestic ritual are a vehicle for passion, anger, despair, whatever human narratives the film-maker is interested in. But this wedding was entirely idyllic. Before the guests sat at the white-covered tables on the lawn they walked out on to a jetty in the lagoon and ate oysters that were fished up out of the water by the ropes they were planted on — this is the method of growing them, tucking the young shells into the strands of a rope — and opened there and then.

Now Etienne greets us with feasts of oysters out of this Etang de Thau. We all stand round and he opens them while we eat them; he eats them too, he's very fast, long practised at the skill of oyster-opening; we all stand bent over slurping them up. The veranda is built of slatted wood so any spills can be hosed through. The oysters are opened and eaten immediately while they are fresh. Large oysters, full of juice, of course not rinsed. And mussels raw as well, opened with a knife instead of by heat. These are delicious too but we don't quite have the habit of them yet.

Ten years ago we went out on the boat, far across the lagoon though the water was only up to our knees, and gathered our own shellfish and shrimps and sea urchins, and on the way back gave their son on his windsurfer a tow back to shore. You eat sea urchins raw too; I tried one, scooping its insides out with a spoon, and could see it was delicious though I didn't quite get into the habit of them either.

With the oysters we drink local wine, and Etienne makes one of his favourite jokes: *le vin d'ici est meilleur que l'eau de là*, which means that the wine from here is better than the water from there, but it's also a pun, on *l'au delà*, the over there, the beyond, the next world. It's a saying to bring in a little nip of mortality to sharpen the pleasures of being alive.

This is the dinner Catherine made. First a pan of warm mussels with a spicy hot sauce to dip them in. Then octopus *à la planche*, literally on a plank, actually grilled on a thick metal plate. Very small ones, with herbs and garlic. And tiny mackerel, cooked in the same way, turned quickly on the sizzling plate. Then *courgette gratin*, followed by cheese, and melons, small sweet round fruit, which we'd picked that evening, cut in half and ate filled with local muscat, if you wanted it.

Catherine apologised for the *gratin*, which she said was too *grillé* and it did look quite burnt actually but it was succulent and juicy underneath and the top crisp and crunchy.

COURGETTE GRATIN

You fry the thinly sliced courgettes with sliced onions in olive oil, put them in a shallow ovenproof dish (hers was the sort of crude brown Spanish pottery you can get cheaply here), sprinkle with a handful of grated Gruyère cheese and bake in a moderately hot oven for half an hour. And don't worry if it seems too *grillé*, it will be delicious.

LA THAUPINIERE

This is the name of the house we are staying in, and another of Etienne's jokes, crossing the name of a mole burrow — *taupe* is a mole, and the reason for the colour called *taupe, la taupinière* its burrow — with the name of the lagoon, Thau. It's a modern house, designed only a few years ago by Etienne, who's an architect, in the shape of a wheel, a not quite complete wheel, with an atrium where the hub would be, and then the spokes radiating out separate the rooms: a kitchen, a dining-room, a wide living-room, bedrooms; on the circumference are the verandas, looking out over the lagoon, and across vines. Steps down from the verandas lead to pink gravel, where we play *boules*. Etienne is pleased when I make a good shot, Cosmo isn't; I think this is very generous of our host, but after a bit I discover it's because we're playing in mixed couples. Cosmo and Catherine win.

It's good to be staying in one place for several days.

DIARY

Sunday morning, 26 June
The weather is stormy — I am sitting looking out across the lagoon towards Sète. Catherine and Etienne went to a wedding in Avignon yesterday and will be back later this morning. The mountain at Sète is very clear, and there are marvellous lurid light patterns in the clouds hanging over it, under a layer of darker grey clouds. The wind is loud in the pine trees nearby. Last night there were storms, thunder and lightning, great forks of it all over the immense sky of this seaside landscape; the stretches of vineyard and lagoon are flat as far as the horizon, so there is great scope for the sky to perform. The grove of pine trees was lit from different angles and showed different colours. The sky was violet and indigo, the gravel terrace ochre, the vines yellowy green. Not the colours of daylight at all.

The electricity failed, and everything was very black. I remembered seeing a candle on the chimney-piece, a candle is a treasure in the black dark. We could sit in its comfortable light and admire the storm. After a while we noticed we could see lights twinkling across the lagoon. Cosmo began to wonder if it was not a blackout but some circuit-breaker triggered by the storm, and so it was, he fiddled in the fuse box and got the lights to come on again. We felt very lucky, to be saved from the stupidity of a night without electricity. How Etienne would have laughed at us.

Just through the pines is Montpenèdre, the house; it's wine from its estate that we've been drinking with the oysters, with a picture on its label of the house and the terrace where we lunched last time. Catherine's brother is the wine-maker, but he doesn't actually tend the grapes, there is a Moroccan man who lives with his family in the farmhouse and looks after the vines and the melons. Yesterday there was a big lunch party in the garden for lawyers, to do with Catherine's sister-in-law; she came over to borrow some hats; a lot of people hadn't come, she said, and when we asked why, she replied, Because they are ill-mannered. It happens a lot now, especially with weddings, people say they will come and don't and so a great deal of expensive food is wasted. Catherine was at a wedding last weekend too and was given quantities of leftover food for her dog, including a great number of little birds made up in small square shapes with their heads stuck back in (quails I presume). There was a *traiteur* doing yesterday's party. We went and had a look just before one o'clock: tables under umbrellas and among the trees, a serving table with great silver bowls of prawns curled over the edge, the centre piled with *bulots de mer*, murky-looking spiral-shelled sea creatures, the insides delicious. They looked like curly marrow bones in the middle of the elegant pink prawns. The centre-piece was a metre wide butterfly made of triangles of bread with smoked salmon and prawns on mayonnaise, a kind of mosaic forming the patterns of the butterfly's wings. I was worried about this; yesterday was a heavy day, the air thick, tense with the thunder that came later. Food can easily 'turn' in such weather; either it doesn't 'take', like mayonnaise, or having taken then goes odd, or off. It was hot there by the house; people were saying that when the sun shines there's always a breeze, but when it is dull the air does not move. The lagoon was certainly leaden, and so was the atmosphere. Today is different, cloudy and breezy with bouts of sunshine.

Behind the serving table of the elegant lunch was a glass refrigerator full of cakes, and to one side a high hearth was built, and on it was roaring a fire of *sarments de vigne*, thick gnarled vine cuttings, to grill the meat. It was going to be a long lunch.

Catherine is a farmer, she owns some of these acres under vines, others under melons, which is how she could build a house here; if she were a holiday-maker or simply a person who wanted to live here she wouldn't be allowed to build. Even owning Montpenèdre, the grand country house with its tall windows and large cool shuttered rooms, they need to employ stratagems for making space for the other sister (the property was divided between the three siblings, which was very hard), building a *caveau* for degustation of the wines of the property and eventually converting it to a dwelling. It is this rustic quality, the earth working, that makes this place so paradisiacal; the vines, the lagoon full of oysters and mussels (conchyculture is the name for all this), the melons. And the houses with their rose gardens and oleanders and coloured pottery urns profiting from the space and industry. Our hosts know they are lucky; they work at being good husbanders of their inheritance.

During the war the Germans occupied Montpenèdre. At the edge of the pine grove is a round concrete object which I supposed to be a septic tank or some such device, but no, it was a gun emplacement, put there by the Nazis to guard the lagoon.

This of course is recent history. It's an ancient place. There have been fisher people along this coast for a long time, living in reed huts, then grouping together in villages. Mèze to one side, a dozen or so kilometres to the east, Marseillan on the other, much the same distance to the west, have been fishing ports since the sixth century BC. Now Etienne and his children go windsurfing and water-skiing and people watch television and own microwaves, but the fishing life goes on. Things change less than they appear to.

How much calmer a life it is for fisher people here than on the Atlantic coast; these are mild and pretty ports compared with the Atlantic slapping at the Port des Pêcheurs at Biarritz, the sea heaving and unfriendly even on a warm and only slightly breezy midsummer day.

Monday, 27 June
The cicadas are the sound of the stillness. A hot day. Etienne and his daughter who came back with them

from Avignon where she works have gone water-skiing, driving off with the skis poking out the top of the 2CV, to a good beach for it, quite some distance away. We're staying here; they wonder a bit at us, of course they don't say anything, that we like to potter round and look at the world, rather than be out doing things in it. We think, fancy driving around in a hot and dusty *deux chevaux* when you could stay here and contemplate all this.

MAGAZINES

Or read magazines. These a great selection of house and garden ones, about south of France houses. The English have always had a particular enthusiasm for Provence which makes them go weak in the knees and silly in the head and admire appallingly patronising books about it by the likes of Peter Mayle, so it's possible to forget that it has a special glamour for the French too; these journals show that to perfection. It is as though Provence is a creation of the imagination, and life there has a magic rhythm of its own.

Apart from having my breath taken by some of the amazing houses in them (funny how infrequently you realise what being really rich can mean) I found a couple of recipes, from a new cookbook by Roger Vergé. Here are my versions of them.

Pommes de terre roties au lauriers

One potato per person — Bintje are good. Cut them partly through in slices 1 cm apart, and push a fresh bay leaf into each slit. Heat oven to 200°C, put in an oiled dish, baste with a tablespoon of oil per potato and twice as much stock. Cook for 40 minutes; they will be melting and golden and all the juice absorbed. This is a good dish to make now that we can get named potatoes for particular purposes.

Tapenade verte aux amandes

Take 250 g green olives, 100 g peeled almonds, 1 tablespoon capers, 6 fillets of anchovy. Purée in a food processor, moistening with olive oil, and a bit of brandy (the original recipe demands *vieux marc*).

This is interesting, but not quite so essential as a straight *tapénade*, made with black olives.

Catherine's meals

Catherine makes lovely simple housewife-of-the-region meals, which is not to say that they're not difficult, or labour intensive, or skilled, but they're not fancy, they are what you cook because this is what people are in the habit of eating round here. Like this lunch.

Anchovies.

Pan-grilled lamb chops with herbs, cooked pink and succulent. (I'd forgotten how good small lamb chops could be until this trip to France.)

St Nectaire, bought on the spot, in its home town in the Auvergne, when they were driving down from Paris last week.

Fruit: peaches, nectarines, apricots, tasting of the sun; ripe flesh as it should be.

No point in eating it otherwise, says Catherine.

I think when I'm allowed just one cheese to take to my desert island I'll choose St Nectaire. It's nutty, sweet, sharp, strong, you'd never tire of it. Especially the kind called *fermier*, of artisanal rather than industrial concoction. It's also one cheese never exported here, maybe because it's not pasteurised. I can't suggest a substitute, though you could replace it with a washed rind cheese.

ANCHOVIES

This is the way Catherine prepared the anchovies. They were fresh, about seven or eight centimetres long. She boned them (this is what I mean about the dishes being simple, not fancy, but not slap-dashily easy — there were a lot of these little fish) and marinated them overnight in lemon juice — lime juice is good too — herbs and a little olive oil. They were superb.

BARBECUE

Another time we have more of the melons from the field beside the house with local raw ham. And one day Etienne cooks lunch: a Toulouse sausage a metre long. He makes a little fire of vine twigs on the gravel, coils the sausage on a four-legged grill which sits over the fire on a small metal tripod-like pole, with notches so you can adjust it up and down. At one point he throws on a handful of dried rosemary which flares and hisses. His daughter berates him: what if a spark flew up, and caught the pine trees, igniting the oily scented haze the sun draws out of them, the whole place would go up. La Thaupinière, Montpenèdre, the whole coast. An inferno. Nonsense, says Etienne, and this time he's right.

FORTIFIED CHURCHES

Our leased car has done enough kilometres to need servicing so we take it into Agde. This town, originally on the spot where the river Hérault runs into the sea, but now further upstream, was founded by the Greeks some two-and-a-half thousand years ago and was called Agathée, as in the English Agatha; then the name contracted to Agde. We leave the car at the garage and walk along the street to the river which is rather mighty at this point and look across it to the cathedral. It's a great bleak black fortress.

There can be something romantic about a fortified town, but a fortified church is a grim paradox and sinister. The brilliant sunshine of the Mediterranean coast shines harsh and unforgiving upon its great blank walls. In the nineteenth century somebody stuck a puny and incongruous door in its west front, but didn't succeed in making it look any more friendly. One of its towers is a keep, and there's a hole in the roof of the vault for defenders to haul up provisions on a rope. As well as vats of oil to boil, and pour through the machicolations, which are platforms protected by the battlements, with holes in the floor through which you could drop large stones or hot lead or the boiling oil, so nobody could get close. The machicolations fit in neatly between the buttresses. At the right time of day you can see where they are because the sun shines through them on to the wall below.

Agde cathedral was rebuilt in the twelfth century around a ninth-century edifice, and owes its form to the persecution of the Albigensian heresy. The cathedral at Albi, the town that gave its name to the heresy, is perhaps the most famous of the fortified churches, with its soaring impregnable walls of rose-pink brick. It's dedicated to St Cecilia, patron saint of organ music. Another is les Saintes Maries de la Mer, deep in the marshy Camargue where the Gypsies live: once again towering windowless walls supported on Romanesque buttresses, linked by arches with machicolations, and a mighty crenellated watch-tower where the reliquaries of the saints, the three holy Marys (black Sara patron saint of the Gypsies is in the crypt) are kept. There's a well in the middle of the nave which makes it very siegeworthy.

All over the south of France are these fortified churches, some wholly so, some with just the tower made strong, some half and half, like St Nazaire at Béziers, which has machicolated arcades and a great rose window ten metres across. These churches took a long time to build; perhaps by the time of the window people felt more secure. The churches fell into the hands of Cathars and Christians alternately, for however powerful these fortresses, they were not impregnable. They continued to come in handy during the Wars of Religion, when the Catholics were fighting the Protestants.

After these unChristian monuments — or should I say, all too Christian — it's a relief to go to Carcassonne, which being heavily fortified itself can afford a cathedral that is a miracle of lightness and grace, with a transept made entirely of glass supported by pillars of awesome slenderness.

They have a terrible plain beauty, those squatting stone fortresses of religion, they brood in their self-containment on a landscape ... I was going to say at last peaceful but maybe not. It's not so long since the Nazis herded all the women and children — 247 children — of Oradour sur Glane into their church and set fire to it. The men were shut in barns and garages. Dynamite was used, machine guns, hand grenades. We shouldn't kid ourselves we've got more civilised than the medieval fortifiers of churches.

MARSEILLAN

On our last night at La Thaupinière we go to a restaurant in Marseillan for dinner, in the old port, and sit outside in the mild bright evening. Had Etienne or I got drunk or merry and tipped our chairs over sideways we'd have fallen into the water. There are fishing boats and pleasure craft and barges tied up; some people disembark from a barge flying a New Zealand flag and ride off on bicycles. The sun sets and the light cools. We eat fish with *aioli*, which was not quite as good as the one this recipe makes; it was too runny.

AIOLI

I make mine in a mortar, first of all crushing 4 (or 5 or 6) garlic cloves (it's easier if you chop them first) then using a small whisk beating in 2 egg yolks. Gradually, drop by drop, add the olive oil; it will probably take a cup or more. When it's really thick add about a teaspoon of vinegar or lemon juice, then a bit more oil; the more you add the thicker it will be. If you lose it, if it turns, start again with another egg yolk and drip the turned mixture in, again slowly.

You can make it in a blender, using the same ingredients but the eggs whole. It will work well, but will not be quite so thick and unctuous. I like it made with a dark greenish oil.

NORTH

We get up early and leave before six. We're going to Sévérac. Another loop. Whenever we can, we come curving back, to this, the most beloved place of all. I wrote *Spider Cup* about it, and a chapter of *Eat My Words*, called 'A Nourishing Landscape', centres upon it. We've lived there for periods of a month and more on a number of occasions, and once the children went to school there. The baker's son fancied Lucy, who was eleven at the time, and sent her little notes saying I love you, in English. They liked that school, and learnt French with a marvellous southern accent, which gives full weight to all its syllables. They could recite a story called *L'enfant et le serpent*, the child and the serpent, which perfectly catches it.

The road from the shores of the Mediterranean up the escarpment to the high country and eventually to Sévérac has collapsed down the cliff in some recent heavy rains, fortunately early in the morning, before dawn, and not when it was heavy with traffic. So we have to take a detour, a back road, a winding narrow frightening but very beautiful set of zigzags up the nearly vertical plateau edge. Then across the bare desert country of the Larzac, which was dangerous territory for pilgrims because of its barrenness and its brigands, until the crusaders, the Templars, the Knights of Malta, fortified a number of villages and made travelling safer. Their remains are still there, often in excellent repair: La Couvertoirade, La Cavalerie, Ste Eulalie de Cernon, we've paid attention to all of them in the past. They are usually things like craft villages and suchlike seducers of tourists nowadays.

By eight o'clock we are driving into Millau, down another escarpment into the valley of the Tarn, which we last met as a wide slow river over in the west at Moissac. We can't see anything of it; the valley is full of mist, only the top of the plateau shows. But Millau is coming alive, the big cafés on the place Mandarous are full of people having breakfast, civil servants a lot of them seem to be in this large provincial town, quite elegant; the fashion this year is for prettily coloured summer sports coats on men, rose pink, green, lemon.

We always make several trips to Millau from Sévérac. It's got a flourishing leather industry which came from making Roquefort out of sheep's milk, and so killing the lambs, which give a most beautiful fine soft skin. There's a museum we went to once to get out of the cold, and found a display of red pottery from Gallo-Roman times; it used to be made here and sent out all over the empire. One unfortunate potter had had a terrible kiln accident, whole shelves had collapsed and all the pots squashed and fused together. The potter had thrown the whole mess away in a hole nearby, probably not being able to bear even to look at it, only to have it dug up intact several thousand years later, and now the complete disaster is displayed for everyone to see; what an irony. Except that for us to see this ancient accident is very moving, especially for me, who nearly became a potter once.

One year I bought a belt in Millau, made of leather, a drive belt for the sewing machine in the house at Sévérac, a curious machine which was built in the 1890s, and still had its instruction book so I could learn how to use it. It was in French but had diagrams to help with the technical words. It had a bobbin shaped like a rocket. I bought some fabric in Albi at a stall opposite the cathedral and made skirts for Lucy and me out of a pattern in a magazine; I've still got mine though it's faded.

INHERITANCE

We arrive in Sévérac at ten o'clock. We know it's there from far off, by the castle on its rock commanding all the countryside around, saying to all comers, This is a place worth having, worth guarding. The valley is warm and full of sunlight, the fields already gold so early in the season. The house with its thick stone walls is still cool, and fresh though it has been shut up for months. It's closed up for most of the year; when you leave at the end of summer you have to turn off the water and then go round and turn on every tap and pour methylated spirits down the plug-holes, because of the danger of the pipes freezing. And then there are several mains switches for the electricity that must be shut off. When you arrive next season you have to undo all this, so it's best not to arrive after dark, or you'll find yourself stumbling through cobwebby cellars by torchlight or even candlelight trying to remember where the switches were last time. And up an attic staircase as well.

Yet you could think Sévérac was an enchanted house, because every time you arrive, there is its familiar smell waiting for you, homely, spicy, cared for, you breathe it in and with it comes … well-being. There doesn't even seem to be any dust. You go and open the shutters and look across at the sloping fields, green in spring and summer, yellowing as the season ages, at the old grey chapel embowered in trees, at the hedgerows I once likened to Gothic spandrels: the line of the hill Gothic, a lovely perpendicular arch spandrelled with hedges, I wrote; quite hard work that image but I stick by it. You breathe in the scented air, listen to the faint tinkle of sheep bells, which they wear to frighten away vipers. The sheep whose lambs are slaughtered so their milk can be made into Roquefort cheese, the skin of the newborn lambs making the famously fine leather for ladies' gloves.

All this I put in *Spider Cup*. People are always asking me is this novel autobiographical, and I say the town is, the castle and the house, they're all there, true, nothing invented. *La cousine*'s heavy white linen, embroidered white on white, that she left to Bernard the grandson of her cousin, along with the house, the copper jam pan, the crocodile now a leather case that's lost its stuffing, all the little bronzes, dogs and maidens and small boys, the cellar full of dust and lumber, the sentimental pictures, the filet net curtain. This curtain: it hangs straight at the window, and on its fine filet grid is embroidered a little boy, playing a double-fluted pipe. He stands on a fountain supported by dolphins, with water drops spraying up in an arc and falling into an ornamental basin. He's a little boy at two removes from reality: a picture of a statue. A boy of stone in thread.

I fell in love with all these things. With the house and its ornaments. With the light across the valley. With the castle and its grim story of the duke who murdered his wife because he believed she was unfaithful to him, and in a penance without remorse built the chapel opposite. With the tinkle of viper-scaring sheep bells. I fell in love, and wrote a novel about them because I wanted to possess them. If you read that book you can see that it is full of desire.

I could write it when I found a modern story to parallel and collide with his, a modern story of jealousy and imagined revenge, a story of women's lives and how to live them, of Gloriande plucked from her brilliant court and murdered, of Elinor the would-be polymathic modern wife of a faithless husband, of *la cousine* Berthe who sewed her trousseau and never married, Berthe who stitched lambskin gloves for a living, and who are we to say she was not content?

HOUSEKEEPING

The first thing we have to do is go shopping. To begin with to Shopy, the supermarket where the glove factory used to be, le Gant Albatros it was called. Couldn't wait to start housekeeping. I miss housekeeping when I've been living in hotels and staying with people, at least I do when Cosmo's there too because housekeeping is so much part of the fabric of our lives together. Shopping, choosing, cooking, sitting at our own table: ours because we've made it so by serving our own food at it.

At Shopy I bought some calf's liver and fried it in a little olive oil with a lot of onions cooked pale, not browned; it was still juicy, if not quite pink, inside its crispy surface, it had that tension to it that marks so much good food, firm yet melting, like scallops barely cooked, or the sublime white asparagus, or *foie gras*.

BRANDADE DE MORUE

We also went to the butcher/*charcutier* and bought some *brandade de morue*, which was delicious, and so it should have been, it was something of a rich person's hobby at seventy-six francs a punnet. No longer the food of the poor. But worth it. The salt cod, the *stockfisch*, that it's made from comes from Norway, brought originally by soldiers fighting in Louis XIV's wars against Holland, but it's claimed much refined by local cooks. In this part of France it's made into a dish called *estofinado* which is supposed to be *patois* for *stockfisch*. The one we buy is called *brandade*, but it could owe its presence here to *estofinado*.

My recipe for *estofinado* says to desalt 2 kg salt cod in running water (a stream or a fountain) for 8 to 10 days, cut in thick slices, cook in water for 3 hours, drain, take out the bones. Cook 500 g potatoes in the same water, then mash them and the fish and mix both together over gentle heat adding hot olive or walnut oil, butter, and 6 hard-boiled eggs; at the moment of serving add another 6 eggs beaten in *crème fraîche*, garlic, parsley, pepper — plenty of all of those, it should be highly seasoned; if it's too dry add some more raw eggs and oil. No other quantities are given, you need to use enough.

You can see it's a magnificent dish. There are some restaurants in Australia which do a *brandade* well, others don't. One that does it superbly is the Bistro Moncur in Sydney; it's one of those dishes you sit and eat in tiny forkfuls and the only word for what you feel is bliss. Moncur's chef Damien Pignolet gave me the recipe he uses at home, which he says is a bit different in presentation from the one in the restaurant but similar in taste and feel.

Soak the salt cod in lots of cold water for 12 hours, changing the water every 3 hours. Drain. Place it into a pan and cover with cold water, bring it slowly to the boil and reduce to a simmer for 2 minutes. Cover the pan and leave off the heat for 5 minutes. Drain well. Remove any bones and place the flesh in a wide bowl. Using two forks pull the fish into threads, rather fine. Add the warm potato purée, mixing lightly.

Heat the oil to about 80°C in one pan and the cream in another to the same temperature. Allow the oil to infuse the garlic at this temperature for 10 minutes. Now slowly work in the oil and cream alternately until an homogeneous texture is achieved and it will stand fairly firm.

Correct the seasoning with pepper, a touch of lemon and the same of nutmeg.

Salt will probably not be required, however taste in the early stages of adding the liquid and add salt then if required. This will give it time to mature.

To serve chop 2 cloves of garlic finely and add some olive oil. Leave this at room temperature for 10 minutes, strain it, discard the garlic and use the oil to fry slices of French bread golden brown.

At home I serve the *brandade* with a criss-cross of anchovy fillets cut in half lengthwise and fried capers. A little fresh parsley won't be lost either.

He ends by wishing *Bon appetit*; I have one already just by reading the recipe.

MARKET

I'm a fan of markets. Maybe it's their tenuousness, their fragility, the difficulty of people getting everything here, setting it up and then taking it all away again, and the street cleaners come in and by early afternoon it's as though it's never been. Mostly the people are the same ones, week after week, with a few extras, and usually they do this six days a week.

It's a hard life, and most of them are extremely cheerful about it.

Sévérac market takes place in the square in front of the railway station, Sévérac Gare, which gives its name to the new (nineteenth-century) town at the foot of the hill, where the land is flat. You can get to the Mediterranean, or Spain, to Paris and beyond, along this railway line, though for most of its life the locals haven't bothered, the next town or two was far enough for them. The market spills out into surrounding streets as well, but I'm not sure what this size means, there seems to be less food than there used to be. Maybe everybody is going to Shopy. Though there are a lot of small stalls with a local farmer or more often his wife selling their produce. We buy a lovely fresh goat's cheese, and some warm sun-scented apricots and peaches, and a bottle of oil grown just down the road in a place as precisely mapped as a wine chateau. We'll use this and leave the rest for Bernard, our main fun is buying it.

There are still cages of birds, guinea fowl, geese, pigeons, and an old woman, bent and thin but full of energy is disputing with the seller, though somehow you can tell she's going to buy, she's just not going to succumb easily, and eventually she hobbles away with a pair of guinea fowl tied by the feet and carried dangling upside down. For the pot? To kill and cook straightaway? To fatten up in the fowl-yard? For breeding? I feel a pang of ignorance; I don't know.

We buy some trout. There's a man selling them out of a basin of water. He fishes one out and kills it with a flick. Fresh trout. The small basin seems a bit cruel. We buy ours off a slab in the fishmonger's van, and cook it in a little of the new olive oil and eat with lemon. Brilliant. The older I get the more I like really simple food, that tastes of itself. *Faites simple*, said Curnonsky.

But a lot of the market isn't food at all. There are racks of clothes, and hats, and shoes, and lots of terrible cheap lace, for curtains, brightly white machine-made stuff and when you look at the filet net hanging in the windows of our house, well, you can see how the old order's changed. Ours is a work of art, and on the way to being a museum piece. And that's rather sad.

The other thing the market is full of: flowers. Stalls and stalls of them, to plant and to put in vases. *Fleurissons nos villes* is a message heeded here, it seems. And plenty of vegetables to plant; I used to wonder why it was always difficult to find good vegetables in Sévérac until I realised everyone must have been growing their own, but that was in the old days.

We've bought some fairly local wine, too. In the evenings we sit in the dining-room, with its casements overlooking the valley, and watch the dusk fall as we eat our trout, our calf's liver, our goat's cheese and apricots, and drink the wine of the land. Some of this comes from Estaing, a small town of rose-coloured stone bridges over the Lot; I find a book about the area and read that the patron saint of Estaing is called Fleuret and that his name-day is a feast of misrule when bad behaviour is licensed and foolishness rules. Another mysterious saint. His is a common name for children in the area, with Fleurette for girls. The youth at the garage in Agde where the car was serviced was called Fleuret, and I remember thinking how romantic, for the name means flowery. Now I wonder if he came from Estaing.

We don't do much in the hot afternoons except sit around in our cool shuttered house and read. Later we go out, climb up to the castle or drive into the countryside. The farmers on their state-of-the-art tractors and hay bailers are making use of the long twilight coolness too, producing no doubt too much food. On one narrow road we follow a flock of sheep, with a woman shepherding them and some dogs, there's nothing to do but crawl along behind until they reach home. We go to Vimenet looking for a fortified church but it's not the one we expect, though plain and beautiful, and open, churches often aren't these days, too many thieves and vandals. A small girl standing on a flowery veranda, she's about three, says *Bonjour* as is the way of people in the country, then pulls up her teeshirt and starts rubbing her tummy in that proud and carefree manner that children have. Children and cats: all over the world they have the same gestures; how do they know them? Proudly rubbing their tummies just comes naturally to small children everywhere. Then they have to learn not to do it.

RED 'R' MEALS

From Sévérac we have two of the most memorable meals of our trip. One is at Meyrueis, at Le Mont Aigoual, which has a red R in the *Michelin*, meaning a good meal for the price, and often regional. We drive from Sévérac down to the River Tarn along a winding road which is straighter than it used to be, still marked by plaques to those who died there, some in car accidents, some fighting in the Resistance. Then along the gorge of the Tarn to the Jonte, and this is the exciting part, for the road follows this gorge, sometimes low down, close to the river, sometimes high up on the almost perpendicular cliffs that drop down to it. The road is a narrow ledge, and it's on my side that the ground plunges away; everybody drives in the middle of the road but sometimes the traffic is two-way so you have to move over. I'm sure Cosmo isn't going to drive off the edge, in fact I'm absolutely convinced of it, nevertheless it's a scary drop down there, especially when you look out the window and can't see the road at all, just the drop. In parts there's a low stone wall along it, which is comforting.

At one point there's a tiny verge, a sort of hump by the side of the road, and there are people set up with telescope, binoculars, cameras; they must be looking at the eagles cruising round the high crags. An easy life for eagles, the hot air rises and they just sit on it, don't have to do any work at all.

There are villages clinging to the side of these cliffs, giving a whole new meaning to the cliché of clinging villages, inhabited, full of geraniums; geraniums the banner of prosperity are flourishing here. The rocks look like the turrets of castles but are rocks. Every now and then the roads dropping off to the villages make the one we are on look like a superhighway. And yet quite flash cars, you can see them, drive down there. Silky scarlet poppies bloom by the way. On a little shady shelf above the road some people are picnicking, an idyllic spot under flowering trees that must belong to an old orchard stepping steeply up the hill.

We come across a sign saying Meyrueis thirty minutes from here which is encouraging since we're short of time but in fact this is dangerously optimistic so we are a bit late for early country lunching. Lucky we've booked, they're still pleased to see us. Anyway, we're very hungry, so we decide for the first time on this trip to take the gastronomic menu instead of the *menu du terroir*, which is seventy francs, the gastronomic 140 (remember I'm dividing by four to convert to dollars, though by the end of our stay the Visa bills show it's more like 3.8, even 3.7). This menu is a great idea, chosen as follows:

M: *fantaisie* of raw ham and sausage (superb local *charcuterie*) with some melon, walnuts, salad, and a confiture of onions.
C: smoked salmon with fresh light cheese, a bit herby, dill probably.
M *and* C: *ragoût de riz d'agneau*, tiny lamb's sweetbreads, smaller than a thumb, a speciality of the

region [Roquefort sheep again] with *écrivisses*, fresh water crayfish, and great luck, they're rare these days. Done in a sauce made with fish *fumet* [which is a reduced stock] and Noilly Prat — herby again.

(We could have had *coquilles St-Jacques* but we've left Compostela behind and anyway the *écrivisses* were not to be missed.)

M: *magret de canard aux épices*, duck breasts, the spices being different sorts of peppercorns, pink, green, black, with juniper berries, all sorts of little round spices. Not so pink as I like, but sightly. Plus *ratatouille*, very fresh, not too cooked.

C: hearty slice of *gigot de mouton*, leg of mutton being hard to come by at home. With a *galette de Roquefort*.

(We clean up our plates, all but lick them; the waitress is impressed.)

M *and* C: cheeses of the region, a great platter to choose from: Roquefort Papillon Carte Noir [the best, very blue and creamy], St Nectaire, *chèvre fermier* [farm-made], a rather brie-like local sheep's cheese. These are the ones we actually eat.

M: nougat with raspberry *coulis*, not ice-cream, solid but light, not frozen or gelatinous.

C: *crème brulée*, a runny chilled cream with a crisp thin slice of dark toffee over the top.

The *menu du terroir*, which means, of the soil, the *terroir* being what makes a Riesling from the Hunter taste different from one grown in the Barossa valley, had *confidou* and a salad with little black puddings; I regretted not having that and comparing it with the one in Agen.

Confiture d'Oignons

This translates as onion jam.

120 g butter
750 g onions sliced
5 g pepper ground
salt
100 g sugar
100 mL sherry vinegar
250 mL red wine

Melt butter in a wide saucepan, add onions, pepper, salt, and sugar. Cover and cook over gentle heat for 30 minutes. Stir frequently with a wooden spoon, watch it doesn't burn, or brown very much.

Add sherry vinegar and red wine. Cook another 30 minutes, uncovered, and continue to stir frequently.

The recipe I adapted this from had grenadine, 30 mL, which could be replaced by *crème de cassis*; these are there for the colour and can be left out, or else a drop of blackcurrant syrup could be used.

Served cold it goes very well with game, and with a terrine of pork. Or you can eat it hot as a vegetable.

After this lunch we feel very good, not at all as though we've eaten too much, the menu must have been well planned, delicately balanced. Designed for human beings, not characters out of Rabelais as sometimes seems the case.

We decide to walk along the river a little, it's a small stream that runs through the centre of the town, and take coffee in a café on a little bridge over it; we've eaten slowly and outstayed everyone else in the restaurant by an hour or more. Coffee and more water; we've already drunk two litres with lunch. And of course we didn't have much wine because of driving.

It is hot, hot, hot. When we get home we discover it was thirty-nine degrees in the gorges today. They concentrate the sun, bounce it off their steep slopes and focus it in the deep valleys. That's why they grow such good fruit there. At le Rosier where the Jonte meets the Tarn we stand on a stone bridge and watch people playing in the clear green water of the river; on the banks are set up small tents among the trees. Blissful summer holiday. We sit on a terrace over the river and drink fresh squeezed lemon juice that we keep filling up with ice-cubes. Anything to get out of a hot car on a hot road. Why aren't we down there disporting in that cool green river? At least when we get back to Sévérac, a different route from this morning's, driving up the side of the gorge in a series of diagonals linked by horseshoe bends, it's the cool of the evening; up in the high plateau country the nights are chill.

Our second memorable meal is at Le Trou de Bozouls at a place called Le Belvédère, on Saturday evening. We've eaten quite a large lunch, trying to finish up everything in the fridge; of course we bought too much, got carried away with our house-keeping.

But we've planned to go and so we drive to Le Trou de Bozouls which really is a big hole in the ground with perpendicular cliffs like Rocamadour and a small river winding round the bottom of it. It's funny to look at these small neat rivers and imagine them carving out such steep and massive holes. There's a church down there too which used to have a stone roof until somebody discovered that it was bowing the walls outwards and put on a wooden one instead, and an ancient monastery or something beside it which is now an old people's home; there are some marvellous buildings turned into old people's homes in France, you'd think that simply living in them would make you content, but probably not.

At Le Belvédère we sit outside in the courtyard where there's some coolness. The view is to be had from inside but it's too hot in there, the proprietor cooks a lot of his dishes on a wood fire in a great stone hearth, it burns down to a powerful glowing heat. We order *à la carte*: *foie gras de canard*, fine, very tense duck livers in a terrine, palpably separate; *magret fumé de canard* (we're getting back towards the Périgord and duck country), the breasts smoked like raw ham. Then Cosmo has *saumon grillé sur feu de bois*, that same wood fire in the dining-room, and my lamb cutlets are cooked on it too, except that they're fillet and not so pink as I'd like, but excellent flavour, the meat juicy and plump. Superb vegetables: green asparagus and a little tart of courgettes.

It's still light when we drive home across the plateau. To bed early, sliding into the cool slippery linen smoothness of *la cousine*'s sheets. Tomorrow we'll get up before dawn and drive to Paris, fast as possible down the motorways. I can choose this moment to say: this is the end of our pilgrimage. We didn't get to Compostela but we spent nearly five days in Sévérac, this place so much the focus of my desire that I have written a whole novel about it and at length in two other books. And now of course this one. This place with its jealous lord who murdered his wife for her faithlessness, sending her he said on a pilgrimage through the forest to a holy shrine, but intercepting her litter with masked men and his surgeon slitting her wrists and ankles so she bled to death; and maybe she was faithless and maybe she wasn't, maybe her mother-in-law who said she was told lies, but the castle where she was duchess and the little town around it have never forgotten her story, it's written in histories and guidebooks and in people's minds, they tell friends and strangers who come to visit, they know a glamorous narrative when they've lived with it all their lives.

Gloriande's pilgrimage to death: that's one kind we've avoided.

The two most important things, I said at the beginning: food and stories. We've eaten some marvellous food, though we can do that at home, in the cities at any rate, and with care in the country, but the stories ... the stories are something else. Architecture, said Victor Hugo, is the handwriting of the human race, and in that handwriting we have read tales of comfort and terror and heart-catching beauty, for Romanesque is the art of stories. Gothic architecture soars like a song, its shapes abstract and trilling as music, but Romanesque is good stories and great ones, homely, comical, fearful, joyous stories, as potent now as when they were first told, as tough as the stone in which they are set, and tomorrow I will begin my return home with my head full of them. To Australia where we are inventing our way of life along with our cuisine, inventing as people always do, taking the work of others and adding that little fizz of genius that makes it our own. Telling ourselves new stories, but not forgetting the old ones, which are still our civilisation. Knowing we need not choose, we can have both.

BIBLIOGRAPHY

Allardice, Pamela. *A Passion for Chocolate*. Harper-Collins, Sydney, 1994.

Arbellot, Simon. *Curnonsky, Prince des gastronomes*. Les Productions de Paris, 1965.

Barthes, Roland. *Mythologies*. Paladin/Granada, London, 1972.

Beeton, *Mrs Household Management*. Ward, Locke & Co.

Brillat-Savarin, Jean-Anthelme. *The Philosopher in the Kitchen*. Trans. Anne Drayton. Penguin, Harmondsworth, 1970.

David, Elizabeth. *French Provincial Cooking*. Penguin, Harmondsworth, 1960.

Guide Michelin France. 85th edition, 1994.

Guides Michelin Vert. Auvergne, Perigord, Paris, Provence, Pyrénées, Causses, Spain.

Halligan, Marion. *Spider Cup*. Penguin, Ringwood, 1990.

La cuisine de Madame Saint-Ange. Editions Chaix, Grenoble, 1977.

Lourdes: Guide du visiteur et du pelerin. Editions Fleurus, 1992.

Mabey, David and Rose. *Jams, Pickles and Chutneys*. Penguin, Harmondsworth, 1989.

Montagne, Prosper. *Larousse Gastronomique*. Hamlyn, London, 1966.

Petit Robert. *Dictonnaire universel des noms propres*. SNL Le Robert, Paris, 1977.

Sentier de Saint-Jacques. *Federation Francais de la randonée pédestre*, Cahors-Roncevaux, Paris, 1992.

Toussaint-Samat, Maguelonne. *History of Food*. Trans. Anthea Bell. Blackwell, Cambridge, 1992.

Zarnecki, George. Art of the Medieval World. Harry N. Abrams, N.Y., 1975.

INDEX